CRITICAL WRITINGS

DOVER THRIFT EDITIONS

James Joyce

DOVER PUBLICATIONS, INC.
MINEOLA, NEW YORK

DOVER THRIFT EDITIONS

GENERAL EDITOR: SUSAN L. RATTINER
EDITOR OF THIS VOLUME: JANET B. KOPITO

Bibliographical Note

This Dover edition, first published in 2018, is a new compilation of essays, letters, and reviews by James Joyce, reprinted from authoritative sources. Because some of the works in this collection are of a fragmentary nature and were not given titles by James Joyce, each work in question will appear as [Untitled Fragment]. A Note has been specially prepared for this edition.

International Standard Book Number

ISBN-13: 978-0-486-82436-9
ISBN-10: 0-486-82436-5

Manufactured in the United States by LSC Communications
82436501   2018
www.doverpublications.com

Note

JAMES JOYCE (BORN in Dublin, 1882; died in Zurich, 1941), is generally thought to be the most dazzling prose stylist of the twentieth century. His major works include the short story collection *Dubliners* (1914), the novel *A Portrait of the Artist as a Young Man* (1916), and the experimental, groundbreaking longer works *Ulysses* (1922) and *Finnegans Wake* (1939), as well as two early volumes of verse—*Chamber Music* (1907) and *Pomes Penyeach* (1927). A contemporary of the Irish Renaissance—a literary revival marked by cultural and political expression in theater, prose, and poetry that included William Butler Yeats, Lady Isabella Gregory, John Millington Synge, Sean O'Casey, and Padraic Colum—James Joyce set out to discover the meaning of his nationality through his art. He both celebrates and ridicules the historical voyage of Ireland, revealing deep love as well as impatience. His achievement lies largely in his uncanny ability to fuse the intimacy of an individual character's private reflections and inner torments with the larger narrative of human history.

In addition to his well-known prose works, James Joyce was a prolific writer of essays and various forms of commentary, including book and theater reviews. This compilation ranges from a consideration of the great Norwegian dramatist Henrik Ibsen ("Ibsen's New Drama") to fragmentary pieces on the nature of tragedy in art (page 117) and the intrusion of censorship into his own literary work (page 127). In "A Suave Philosophy," Joyce briefly reviews a book about the relationship of Buddhism to the Burmese people; in "Unequal Verse," he assails a book of poetry as a "farrago of banal epics"; and in "The Centenary of Charles Dickens," Joyce reviews the strengths of the Victorian author while noting how he falls short when compared to the "stern realism" and "ultra-modern tendency" of the towering figures of Tolstoy and Zola.

Any reader interested in rounding out an appreciation of the keen literary sensibility, sharp wit, and honesty of James Joyce will benefit from the diverse and entertaining thoughts and impressions that Joyce reveals in the three dozen pieces in this collection.

Contents

CRITICAL WRITINGS

TRUST NOT APPEARANCES

AMDG

THERE IS NOTHING so deceptive and for [all] that so alluring as a good surface. The sea, when beheld in the warm sunlight of a summer's day; the sky, blue in the faint and amber glimmer of an Autumn sun, are pleasing to the eye: but, how different the scene, when the wild anger of the elements has waked again the discord of Confusion, how different the ocean, choking with froth & foam, to the calm, placid sea, that glanced and rippled merrily in the sun. But the best examples of the fickleness of appearances are:—Man and Fortune. The cringing, servile look; the high and haughty mien alike conceal the worthlessness of the character. Fortune that glittering bauble, whose brilliant shimmer has allured and trifled with both proud and poor, is as wavering as the wind. Still however, there is a "something" that tells us the character of man. It is the eye. The only traitor that even the sternest will of a fiendish villian [sic] cannot overcome. It is the eye that reveals to man the guilt or innocence, the vices or the virtues of the soul. This is the only exception to the proverb "Trust not appearances." In every other case the real worth has to be searched for. The garb of royalty or of democracy are but the shadow that a "man" leaves behind him. "Oh! how unhappy is that poor man that hangs on princes' favours." The fickle tide of ever-changing Fortune brings with it—good and evil. How beautiful it seems as the harbinger of good and how cruel as the messenger of ill! The man who waits on the

1

temper of a King is but a tiny craft in that great ocean. Thus we see the hollowness of appearances. The hypocrite is the worst kind of villian [*sic*] yet under the appearance of virtue he conceals the worst of vices. The friend, who is but the fane of fortune, fawns and grovells [*sic*] at the feet of wealth. But the man, who has no ambition, no wealth, no luxury save Contentment cannot hide the joy of happiness that flows from a clear conscience & an easy mind.

LDS.

James A. Joyce

[UNTITLED FRAGMENT]

—BOTH QUESTIONS OF moment and difficult to answer. And although it is, in the main, evident that the conquest gained in a righteous war, is itself righteous, yet it will not be necessary to digress into the regions of political economy, etc, but it will be as well to bear in mind, that all subjugation by force, if carried out and prosecuted by force is only so far successful in breaking mens' [sic] spirits and aspirations. Also that it is, in the extreme, productive of ill-will and rebellion, that it is, again, from its beginning in unholy war, stamped with the stamp of ultimate conflict. But indeed it seems barbaric to only consider subjugation, in the light of an oppressing force, since we shall see that more often is it an influence rather than a positive power, and find it better used than for the vain shedding of blood.

In the various grades of life there are many homely illustrations of its practice—none the truer, that they are without blaze or notoriety, and in the humblest places. The tiller who guides the plough through the ground, and breaks the "stubborn glebe" is one. The gardener who prunes the wayward vine or compels the wild hedge into decent level, subjugating the savage element in "trim gardens," is another. Both of these represent subjugation by force; but the sailor's method is more diplomatic. He has no plough to furrow the resisting wind, nor no knife to check the rude violence of storm. He cannot, with his partial skill, get the better of its unruliness. When Æolus has pronounced his fiat, there is no direct counter-manding his order. That way the sailor cannot overcome him;

3

but by veering, and patient trial, sometimes using the strength of the Wind, sometimes avoiding it, now advancing and now retreating, at last the shifting sails are set for a straight course, and amid the succeeding calm the vessel steers for port. The miller's wheel which although it restrains the stream yet allows it to proceed on its own way, when it has performed the required service, is an useful example. The water rushing in swift stream, is on the higher mountains a fierce power both to excite emotion and to flood the fields. But the magic miller changes its humour, and it proceeds on its course, with all its tangled locks in orderly crease, and laps its waves, in placid resignation, on the banks that slope soberly down from suburban villas. And more, its strength has been utilised for commercial ends, and it helps to feed, with fine flour and bread, no longer the poetical but the hungry.

After these subjugations of the elements, we come to the subjugation of animals. Long ago in Eden responsible Adam had a good time. The birds of the air and the beasts of the field, ministered to his comfort. At his feet slept the docile lion, and every animal was his willing servant. But when sin arose in Adam—before only a latent evil—and his great nature was corrupted and broken, there were stirred up also among beasts the unknown dregs of ferocity. A similar revolt took place among them against man, and they were no longer to be friendly servants but bitter foes to him. From that hour, in greater or less degree, more in one land than another, they have struggled against him and refused him service. Aided often by great strength they fought successfully. But at length by superior power, and because he was man and they were but brutes, they, at least to a great extent, were overcome. Some of them, as the dog, he made the guardians of his house; others, as the horses and oxen, the helpmates of his toils. Others again he could not conquer but merely guard against, but one race in particular threatened by its number and power, to conquer him; and here it may be as well to follow the fate of it and see how a superior power intervened to preserve for man his title, not in derision, of lord of the creation and to keep him safe from the fear of mammoth and of mastodon.

The Zoo elephants are sorry descendants of those mighty monsters who once traversed the sites of smoky cities; who roamed in hordes, tameless and fearless, proud in their power, through fruitful regions and forests, where now are the signs of busy men and the monuments of their skill and toil; who spread themselves over whole continents and carried their terror to the north and south, bidding defiance to man that he could not subjugate them; and finally in the wane of their day, though they knew it not, trooped up to the higher regions of the Pole, to the doom that was decreed for them. There what man could not subdue, was subdued, for they could not withstand the awful changes that came upon the earth. Lands of bright bloom, by degrees, lost all beauty and promise. Luxuriance of trees and fulness of fruit gradually departed, and were not, and stunted growth of shrub and shrivelled berries that no suns would ripen, were found in their room. The tribes of the Mammoth were huddled together, in strange wonder, and this devastation huddled them still closer. From oases, yet left them, they peered at the advancing waves, that locked them in their barren homes. Amid the gradual ice and waters, they eked out the days of the life of their vanity and when nothing remained for them but death, the wretched animals died in the unkind cold of enduring winter, and to-day their colossal tusks and ivory bones, are piled in memorial mounds, on the New Siberian Islands. This is all of them that is left, that man may have good by their death, whom he was not able to make his slaves when they lived, to tempt his greed across the perilous, Polar seas, to those feasts of the wealth of bygone times, that are strewn and bleaching beneath the desolate sky, white and silent through the song of the changeless waves, and on the verge of the eternal fathoms. What a subjugation has this been—how awful and how complete! Scarce the remembrance of the mammoth remains and no more is there the fear of the great woolly elephant but contempt of his bulk and advantage of his unweildiness [sic].

It is generally by intercourse with man, that animals have been tamed and it is noticeable that the domestic tabby and the despised pig rage in distant lands, with all their inbred fierceness and strength. These with others are subjugated by constant war, or driven from familiar haunts, and then their race dies out as the bison of America is dying. Gradually all common animals are subdued to man's rule, becoming once again his servants and regaining something of former willingness, in the patient horse and faithful dog. In some instances the vain-glory and conscious victory of the three spears is observed. Thus, in the swampy marshes of South America, the venomous snakes are lulled into deadness, and lie useless and harmless, at the crooning of the charmer and in shows and circuses before large crowds, broken-spirited lions and in the streets the ungraceful bears are witnesses to the power of man.

It may be that the desire to overcome and get the mastery of things, which is expressed in man's history of progress, is in a great measure responsible for his supremacy. Had it been that he possessed no such desire, the trees and vegetation would have choked the sunlight from him, barring all passage; the hills and seas would have been the bounds of his dwellings; the unstemmed mountain-stream would always snatch away his rude huts and the ravaging hungry beasts stamp on the ashes of his fire. But his superior mind overcame all obstacles, not however universally, for in those places where his visits were seldom, the lower creation has usurped his Kingdom, and his labour must be anew expended in hunting the savage tiger through the jungles and forests of India, and in felling the trees in Canadian woods.

The next important subjugation is that of race over race. Among human families the white man is the predestined conqueror. The negro has given way before him, and the red men have been driven by him out of their lands and homes. In far New Zealand the sluggish Maoris in conceded sloth, permit him to portion out and possess the land of their fathers. Everywhere that region and sky allow, he has gone. Nor any longer does he or may he practise the abuse of subjugation— slavery, at least in its most degrading forms or at all so generally. Yet slavery only seems to have appealed to the conscience of men when most utterly base and inhuman and minor offences never troubled them. Happily this could not continue and now any encroachment on the liberties of others whether by troublesome Turk or not, is met with resolute opposition and just anger. Rights when violated, institutions set at nought, privileges disregarded, all these, not as shibboleths and war-cries, but as deep-seated thorough realities, will happily always call forth, not in foolish romantic madness nor for passionate destruction, but with unyielding firmness of resistance, the energies and sympathies of men to protect them and to defend them.

Hitherto we have only treated of man's sub-

. . .

often when a person gets embarked on a topic which in its vastness almost completely swallows up his efforts, the subject dwarfs the writer; or when a logician has to treat of great subjects, with a view to deriving a fixed theory, he abandons the primal idea and digresses into elaborate disquisitions, on the more inviting portions of his argument. Again in works of fancy, a too prolific imagination literally flys [sic] away with the author, and lands him in regions of loveliness unutterable, which his faculties scarcely grasp, which dazzles his senses, and defies speech, and thus his compositions are beautiful indeed, but beautiful with the cloudiness and dream-beauty of a visionary. Such a thing as this often affects poets of high, fanciful temper, as Shelley, rendering their poetry vague and misty. When however the gift—great and wonderful—of a poetic sense, in sight and speech and feeling, has been subdued by vigilance and care and has been prevented from running to extremes, the true and superior spirit, penetrates more watchfully into sublime and noble places, treading them with greater fear and greater wonder and greater reverence, and in humbleness looks up into the dim regions, now full of light, and interprets, without mysticism, for men the great things that are hidden from their eyes, in the leaves of the trees and in the flowers, to console them, to add to their worship, and to elevate their awe. This result proceeds from the subjugation of a great gift, and indeed it is so in all our possessions. We improve in strength when we husband it, in health when we are careful of it, in power of mental endurance when we do not over-tax it. Otherwise in the arts, in sculpture and painting, the great incidents that engross the artist's attention would find their expression, in huge shapelessness or wild daubs; and in the ear of the rapt musician, the loveliest melodies outpour themselves, madly, without time or movement, in chaotic mazes, "like sweet bells jangled, out of tune and harsh."

It has been pointed out what an influence this desire of man to overcome has exerted over the Kingdom of animals and vegetation, and how it not merely destroys and conquers the worse features but betters and improves what is good. There are spots on this earth, where licence of growth holds absolute sway, where leaves choke the light and rankness holds the soil, where there are dangerous reptiles and fierce beasts, all untamed, amid surroundings of great beauty, in colour and fertility, but overshadowed by the horror of savage unrule. But the coming of man in his onward way, shall alter the face of things, good himself rendering good his own dominions. As has been written—"when true servants of Heaven shall enter these Edens and the Spirit of God enter with them, another spirit will also be breathed into the physical air; and the stinging insect and venomous snake and poisonous tree, pass away before the power of the regenerate human soul"—This is the wished subjugation that must come in good time. And meanwhile we have considered the power of overcoming man, against the lowest races of the world, and his influence in the subjugation of his own mental faculties, and there remains for us to consider the manifold influence of his desire to conquer, over his human instincts, over his work and business and over his reason.

In the sagas of Norway, in ancient epics in the tales of "Knights and barons bold" and to-day in the stories of Hall Caine, we have abundant examples of the havoc that men's

passions make, when they are allowed to spend their force in
Bersirk freedom. Of course in conventional life there are fewer
instances of such characters as Thor, Ospakar, Jason, and Mylrea
as in those savage places which were once their homes. Modern
civilisation will not permit such wholesale licence, as the then
state of affairs gave occasion to. The brood of men now, in
towns and cities, is not of fierce passion, at least not to such
an extent as to make men subserve their rages. The ordinary
man has not so often to guard against fits of demon's anger,
though the Vendetta is still common in Southern Europe but
mankind has quite as many opportunities of subjugating himself
or herself as before. The fretful temper, the base interpretation,
the fool's conceitedness, the fin-de-siècle sneer, the gossiping,
the refusal of aid, the hurting word and worthless taunt, together
with ingratitude and the forgetting of friends—all these are
daily waiting for us to subjugate. Above all, the much-maligned,
greatest charity, so distinct from animal profusion and reckless
liberality, that charitable deeds do not wholly constitute; but
which springs from inner wells of gentleness and goodness;
which is shy of attributing motives; "which interprets everything
for the best;" which dictates, from emotions of Heaven's
giving, the sacrifice of all that is dear, in urgent need, which
has its being and beauty from above; which lives and thrives
in the atmosphere of thoughts, so upraised and so serene that
they will not suffer themselves to be let down on earth among
men, but in their own delicate air "intimate their presence
and commune with themselves"—this utter unselfishness in
all things, how does it on the contrary, call for constant practice
and worthy fulfilling!

Again in the case of man's mission, marked out for him
from the gate of Eden, labour and toil, has not subjugation a
direct influence, with advantage both to the world and to the
man himself. "Foul jungles" says Carlyle "are cleared away,
fair seedfields rise instead and stately cities, and withal
the man

. . .

greater difficulty for some to subjugate their reason, than their passions. For they pit the intellect and reason of men, with their vain theorisings, against the superhuman logic of belief. Indeed to a rightly constituted mind the bugbears of infidelity have no terrors and excite no feeling save contempt. Men have passions and reason, and the doctrine of licence is an exact counterpart of the doctrine of freethinking. Human reason has no part in wisdom, if it fulfils not the whole three attributes given by the inspired writer, if it is not "pudica, pacifica et desursum"—chaste, peaceful and from above. How can it thrive if it comes not from the seat of Wisdom but has its source elsewhere? And how can earthly intellects, if they blind their eyes to wisdom's epithets "pudica, pacifica et desursum" hope to escape that which was the stumbling-block with Abelard and the cause of his fall.

The essence of subjugation lies in the conquest of the higher. Whatever is nobler and better, or reared upon foundations more solid, than the rest, in the appointed hour, comes to the appointed triumph. When right is perverted into might, or more properly speaking, when justice is changed to sheer strength, a subjugation ensues—but transient not lasting. When it is unlawful, as too frequently in the past it has been, the punishment invariably follows in strife through ages. Some things there are no subjugation can repress and if these preserve, as they do and will, the germs of nobility, in good men and saintly lives, they preserve also for those who follow and obey, the promise of after victory and the solace and comfort of active expectation. Subjugation is "almost of the essence of an empire and when it ceases to conquer, it ceases to be." It is an innate part of human nature, responsible, in a great way, for man's place. Politically it is a dominant factor and a potent power in the issues of nations. Among the faculties of men it is a great influence, and forms part of the world's laws, unalterable and for ever—subjugation with the existence also of freedom, and even, within its sight, that there may be constant manifestation of power over all, bringing all things under sway, with fixed limits and laws and in equal regulation, permitting the prowl

. . .

power for force and of persuasion for red conquest, has brought about the enduring rule foretold, of Kindness over all the good, for ever, in a new subjugation.

—The End—

written by
Jas. A. Joyce
27/9/98

THE STUDY OF LANGUAGES

IN THE CHURCH of San' Maria Novella there are seven figures by Memmi, named the seven earthly Sciences. Reading from right to left, the first is the "Art of Letters" and the seventh "Arithmetic." The first is oftener called Grammar, because it refers more directly to that branch of "Letters." Now the artist's idea in this arrangement was to shew the gradual progress from Science to Science, from Grammar to Rhetoric, from Rhetoric to Music and so on to Arithmetic. In selecting his subjects he assumes two things. First he assumes that the primary Science is Grammar, that is, that Science which is the first and most natural one to man, and also that Arithmetic is the last, not exactly as the culmination of the other six, but rather as the final, numbered expression of man's life. Secondly, or perhaps first, he assumes that Grammar, or Letters, is a Science. His first assumption classes, if it does nothing more, Grammar and Arithmetic together as the first and last things in human knowledge. His second assumption, as we have said, makes Grammar a science. Both of these assumptions are directly opposed to the opinions of many illustrious followers of Arithmetic, who deny that "Letters" is a science, and seem or affect to regard it as a totally different thing from Arithmetic. Literature is only at the root a science, that is in its Grammar and Characters, but such conduct is most senseless on the part of the Arithmeticians.

We hope that they will grant that it is essential for a man, who wishes to communicate in the ordinary way with his fellow-man, that he should know how to speak. We, on our part, will admit that, for the building of an intellectual man, his most important study is that of Mathematics. It is the study which most developes his mental precision and accuracy, which gives him a zest for careful and orderly method, which equips him, in the first place, for an intellectual career. We, the pluralised essayist, say this, who were never an ardent votary of the subject, rather from disinclination to taskwork than because of a rooted aversion to it. In this we are supported by the great lights of the age, though Matthew Arnold has his own little opinion about the matter, as he had about other matters. Now while the advocates of more imaginative pursuits fully recognise the paramount importance of a mathematical education, it is deplorable that so many followers of the more rigid course, having assimilated unto themselves, a portion of the rigidity of that course, and a share of its uncompromising theorems, affect to regard the study of languages as altogether beneath them, and merely a random, occasional sort of study. Linguists must be allowed to make protest against such treatment and surely their defence is worthy of consideration.

For that which ennobles the study of Mathematics in the eyes of the wise, is the fact that it proceeds with regular course, that it is a science, a knowledge of facts, in contradistinction to literature, which is in the more elegant aspect of it, imaginary and notional. This draws a line of stern demarcation between the two; and yet as Mathematics and the Sciences of Numbers partake of the nature of that beauty which is omnipresent, which is expressed, almost noiselessly, in the order and symmetry of Mathematics, as in the charms of literature; so does literature in turn share in the neatness and regularity of Mathematics. Moreover we do not, by any means, suffer such a premiss to pass unchallenged, but before taking up the cudgels on behalf of Language and Literature, we wish it to be understood that we admit that the most important study for the mind is Mathematics, and our vindication of Literature will never venture to put it before Mathematics in that respect.

The statement the study of Languages is to be despised since it is imaginary and does not deal with facts nor deals in a precise way with ideas, is absurd. First, because the study of any language must begin at the beginning and must advance slowly and carefully, over ascertained ground. The Grammar of a language, its orthography and etymology are admitted as known. They are studies in the same manner as tables in Arithmetic, surely and accurately. Some will admit this but go on to say that thus far a language is to be approved of, but that the higher parts of syntax and style and history, are fanciful and imaginative. Now the study of languages is based on a mathematical foundation, and sure of its footing, and in consequence both in style and syntax there is always present a carefulness, a carefulness bred of the first implantings of precision. So they are no mere flourishings of unkempt, beautiful ideas but methods of correct expression ruled and directed by clear regulations, sometimes of facts, sometimes of ideas. And when of ideas their expression elevated from the hardness, which is sufficient for "flat unraised" statements, by an over-added influence of what is beautiful in pathetic phrases, swelling of words, or torrents of invective, in tropes and varieties and figures, yet preserving even in moments of the greatest emotion, an innate symmetry.

Secondly even if we [were] disposed to admit, which we are far from doing, that unwarrantable "since" of the mathematicians we should not admit that poetry and imagination, though not so deeply intellectual, are to be despised and their names to be cast out, totally. Are our libraries to contain only works of Science? Are Bacon and Newton to monopolise our shelves? and no place be found for Shakespeare and Milton? Theology is a Science, yet will either Catholic or Anglican, however profound and learned, taboo poetry from their studies, and the one banish a living, constant element of his Church and the other forbid the "Christian Year"? The higher grades of language, style, syntax, poetry, oratory, rhetoric, are again the champions and exponents, in what way soever, of Truth. So in the figure of Rhetoric in Santa Maria's church Truth is seen reflected in a Mirror. The notion of Aristotle and his school, that in a bad cause there can be true oratory, is utterly false. Finally, if they claim, Science advances more the civilization of the world, there must be some restriction imposed. Science may improve yet demoralise. Witness Dr Benjulia. Did the great Science of Vivisection improve him? "Heart and Science"! yes, there is great danger in heartless science, very great danger indeed, leading only to inhumanity. Let it not be our case to stand like him, crushed and broken, aloof from sympathy at the door of his laboratory, while the maimed animals flee away terrified between his legs, into the darkness. Do not think that Science, human or divine, will effect on the one hand a great substantial change for good in men and things, if it merely consults the interests of men in its own interests, and does good to them it may do good to itself, and in everything passes over that first, most natural aspect of man, namely, as a living being, and regard him as an infinitely small actor, playing a most uninteresting part in the drama of worlds. Or on the other hand, if it proceeds, when directed towards divine objects, as a contrivance useful for extracting hard, rational inferences, ever induce in man an uplifting of trust and worship.

Having thus got rid of the obnoxious mathematicians, something is to be said about the study of languages and there chiefly in the study of our own. First, in the history of words there is much that indicates the history of men, and in comparing the speech of to-day day with that of years ago, we have a useful illustration of the effect of external influences on the very words of a race. Sometimes they have changed greatly in meaning, as the word "villain" because of customs now extinct, and sometimes the advent of an overcoming power may be attested by the crippled diction, or by the complete disuse of the original tongue, save in solitary, dear phrases, spontaneous in grief or gladness. Secondly, this knowledge tends to make our language purer and more lucid, and therefore tends also to improve style and composition. Thirdly, the names we meet in the literature of our language are handed down to us, as venerable names, not to be treated lightly but entitled beforehand to our respect. They are landmarks in the transition of a language, keeping it inviolate, directing its course straight on like an advancing way, widening and improving as it advances but staying always on the high road, though many byways branch off it at all parts and seem smooth to follow. Thus these names, as those of the masters of English, are standards for imitation and reference, and are valuable because their use of the language was also based on their study of it, and is for that reason deserving of great and serious attention. Fourthly, and this is the greatest of all, the careful study of the language, used by these men, is almost the only way to gain a thorough knowledge of the power and dignity, that are in the elements of a language and further to understand, as far as nature allows, the feelings of great writers, to enter into their hearts and spirits, to be admitted, by privilege, into the privacy of their proper thoughts. The study of their language is useful as well, not merely to add to our reading and store of thought, but to add to our vocabulary and imperceptibly to make us sharers in their delicateness or strength. How frequently it happens that when persons become excited, all sense of language seems to forsake them, and they splutter incoherently and repeat themselves, that their phrases may have more sound and meaning. Look, how great the difficulty that many have in expressing their most ordinary ideas in correct English. If it were only to rectify these errors which exist amongst us, the study of our language should recommend itself to us. How much more so, then, when it not alone cures these defects, but works such wonderful changes in our speech by the mere contact with good diction and introduces us to beauties, which cannot here be enlarged on but obtain only passing mention, to which our former ignorance or negligence denied us access.

Lest we should seem to dwell overlong [on] our own language let us consider the case of the classics. In Latin—for the writer acknowledges humbly his ignorance of Greek—a careful and well-directed study must be very advantageous. For it acquaints us with a language, which has a strong element in English, and thus makes us know the derivations of many words, which we then apply more correctly and which have therefore a truer meaning for us. Again Latin is the recognised language of scholars and philosophers, and the weapon of the learned; whose books and thoughts are only open, through the medium of translation. Further, it is astonishing that Latin is like Shakespeare in everyone's mouth, without his seeming, in the least, to recognise the fact. Quotations are constantly employed, even by those who are not Latin scholars and common convenience would prompt us to study it. Then also it is the uniform language of the ritual of the Church. Moreover it is for those who study it a great help intellectually, for it has some terse expressions, that are more forcible than many of our similar expressions. For instance a single Latin phrase or word is so complex in meaning, and enters into the nature of so many words, and has yet a delicate shade of its own, that no single word in English will properly represent. Thus Vergil's Latin is said to be so idiomatic as to defy translation. Evidently careful rendering of such language into suitable English must be a great exercise in judgment and expression, if we were to count nothing else. But Latin besides being in its degraded form the language of schoolmen, is in a better form the language of Lucretius, Vergil, Horace, Cicero, Pliny and Tacitus, all of whom are great names and who have withstood dislodgment from their high seats for thousands of years—a fact which is sufficient in itself to gain them a reading. They are moreover interesting as the writers in a vast Republic, the greatest and vastest the world has seen, a Republic which during five hundred years was the home of nearly all the great men of action in that time, which made its name heard from Gibraltar to Arabia, and to the stranger-hating Briton, everywhere a name of power, and everywhere with conquest in its army's van.

ROYAL HIBERNIAN ACADEMY
"ECCE HOMO"

MUNKACSY'S PICTURE WHICH has been exhibited in the principal cities of Europe, is now on view at the Royal Hibernian Academy. With the other two pictures "Christ before Pilate" and "Christ on Calvary" it forms almost a complete trilogy of the later portion of the Passion. Perhaps what strikes one most in the picture under consideration is the sense of life, the realistic illusion. One could well fancy that the men and women were of flesh and blood, stuck into silent trance, by the warlock's hand. Hence the picture is primarily dramatic, not an execution of faultless forms, or a canvas reproduction of psychology. By drama I understand the interplay of passions; drama is strife, evolution, movement, in whatever way unfolded. Drama exists as an independent thing, conditioned but not controlled by its scene. An idyllic portrait or an environment of haystacks do not constitute a pastoral drama, no more than rhodomontade, and a monotonous trick of "tutoyer" build up a tragedy. If there be only quiescence in one, or vulgarity in the second, as is generally the case, then in neither one nor the other is the note of true drama sounded for a moment. However subdued the tone of passions may be, however ordered the action or commonplace the diction, if a play, or a work of music, or a picture concerns itself with the everlasting hopes, desires and hates of humanity, or deals with a symbolic presentment of our widely related nature, albeit a phase of that nature, then it is drama. Maeterlinck's characters may be, when subjected to the search-light of that estimable torch, common sense,

unaccountable, drifting, fate-impelled creatures—in fact, as
our civilisation dubs them, uncanny. But in whatever dwarfed
and marionette-like a manner, their passions are human, and
so the exposition of them is drama. This is fairly obvious
when applied to a stage subject but when the word drama is
in an identical way, applied to Munkacsy, it may need perhaps
an additional word of explanation.

In the statuary art the first step towards drama was the
separation of the feet. Before that sculpture was a copy of the
body, actuated by only a nascent impulse, and executed by
routine. The infusion of life, or its semblance, at once brought
soul into the work of the artist, vivified his forms and elucidated
his theme. It follows naturally from the fact that the sculptor
aims at producing a bronze or stone model of man, that his
impulse should lead him to the portrayal of an instantaneous
passion. Consequently although he has the advantage of the
painter, in at the first glance deceiving the eye, his capability
to be a dramatist is less broad than the painter's. His power of
moulding can be equalised by the painter's backgrounds and
skilful disposition of shades, and while in such a manner
naturalism is produced on an areal canvas, the colours, which
add another life, help his theme to its expression in a very much
completer and clearer whole. Moreover, and this applies
markedly in the present case, as the theme becomes loftier or
more extended, it can manifestly obtain more adequate treatment
in a large picture than in the crowding of colourless, perfectly-
modelled statues in a tableau. Notably then does the difference
hold in the instance of "Ecce Homo" where some seventy
figures are limned on one canvas. It is a mistake to limit drama
to the stage; a drama can be painted as well as sung or acted,
and "Ecce Homo" is a drama.

In addition, it is much more deserving of the comment of a
dramatic critic than the majority of the pieces which are directly
under his notice in the theatre. To speak of the technical point
of an artwork such as this is, to my thinking, somewhat
superfluous. Of course the draping, and the upraised hands,
and outstretched fingers reveal a technique and a skill, beyond
criticism. The narrow yard is a scene of crowded figures, all

drawn with a master's faithfulness. The one blemish is the odd, strained position of the governor's left hand. It gives one the impression of being maimed or crippled from the manner in which the cloak conceals it. The background is a corridor, opened on the spectator, with pillars upholding a verandah, on which the eastern shrubs show out against a sapphire sky. At the right hand and in the extreme corner, as you face the picture, a stairway of two flights, say some twenty steps in all leads to a platform which is thus almost at right angles to the line of the pillars. The garish sunlight falls directly over this platform leaving the rest of the court partly in the shade. The walls are decorated and at the back of the piazza is a narrow doorway crowded with Roman soldiery. The first half of the mob, that is, those next underneath the platform, is enclosed between the pillars and a swinging chain in the foreground, which is parallel to them. A decrepit street cur, the only animal in the picture, is crouching by it. On the platform in front of the soldiers, stand two figures. One has his hands bound in front and is standing facing the rabble, his fingers just touching the balustrade. A red mantle is so placed about the shoulders as to cover the entire back and a little of the foreshoulders and arms. The whole front of the figure is thus exposed to the waist. A crown of irregular, yellowish thorns is on the temples and head and a light, long reed barely supported between the clasped hands. It is Christ. The other figure is somewhat nearer the populace and leans a little towards them over the balustrade. The figure is pointing at Christ, the right arm in the most natural position of demonstration, and the left arm extended in the peculiar, crippled way I have already noticed. It is Pilate. Right underneath these two main figures, on the paved yard, is the tossing, tumbling Jewish rabble. The expressions conveyed in the varying faces, gestures, hands and opened mouths are marvelous. There is the palsied, shattered frame of a lewd wretch; his face is bruted animalism, feebly stirred to a grin. There is the broad back and brawny arm and tight clenched fist, but the face of the muscular "protestant" is hidden. At her [sic] feet, in the angle where the stairway bends a woman is kneeling. Her face is dragged in an unwholesome pallor but quivering with emotion. Her beautifully rounded arms are displayed as a contrast of writhing pity against the brutality of the throng. Some stray locks of her copious hair are blown over them and cling to them as tendrils. Her expression is reverential, her eyes are straining up through her tears. She is the emblem of the contrite, she is the new figure of lamentation as against the severe, familiar types, she is of those, the sorrowstricken, who weep and mourn but yet are comforted. Presumably, from her shrinking pose, she is a magdalen. Near her is the street dog, and near him a street urchin. His back is turned but both arms are flung up high and apart in youthful exultation, the fingers pointing outwards, stiff and separate.

In the heart of the crowd is the figure of a man, furious at being jostled by a well clad Jew. His eyes are squinting with rage, and an execration foams on his lips. The object of his rage is a rich man, with that horrible cast of countenance, so common among the sweaters of modern Israël. I mean, the face whose line runs out over the full forehead to the crest of the nose and then recedes in a similar curve back to the chin, which, in this instance is covered with a wispish, tapering beard. The upper lip is raised out of position, disclosing two long, white teeth, while the whole lower lip is trapped. This is the creature's snarl of malice. An arm is stretched forth in derision, the fine, snowy linen falling back upon the forearm. Immediately behind is a huge face, with features sprawled upon it, the jaws torn asunder with a coarse howl. Then there is the half profile and figure of the triumphant fanatic. The long gaberdine falls to the naked feet, the head is erect, the arms perpendicular, raised in conquest. In the extreme end is the bleared face of a silly beggar. Everywhere is a new face. In the dark hoods, under the conical headresses [sic], here hatred, there the mouth gaping open at its fullest stretch, the head thrown back on the nape. Here an old woman is hastening away, horrorstruck, and there is a woman of comely appearance but evidently a proletariat. She has fine, languid eyes, full features and figure, but marred with crass stupidity and perfect, if less revolting bestiality. Her child is clambering about her knees, her infant hoisted on her shoulder. Not even these are free from the all pervading aversion and in their small beady eyes twinkles the fire of rejection, the bitter unwisdom of their race. Close by are the two figures of John and Mary. Mary has fainted. Her face is of a grey hue, like a sunless dawn, her features rigid but not drawn. Her hair is jet black, her hood white. She is almost dead, but her force of anguish keeps her alive. John's arms are wound about her, holding her up, his face is half feminine in its drawing, but set in purpose. His rust coloured hair falls over his shoulders, his features express solicitude and pity. On the stairs is a rabbi, enthralled with amazement, incredulous yet attracted by the extraordinary central figure. Round about are the soldiers. Their mien is self-possessed contempt. They look on Christ as an exhibition and the rabble as a pack of unkennelled animals. Pilate is saved from the dignity his post would have given him, by the evidence that he is not Roman enough to spurn them. His face is round, his skull compact, the hair cropped short on it. He is shifting, uncertain of his next move, his eyes wide open in mental fever. He wears the white and red Roman toga.

It will be clear from all this that the whole forms a wonderful picture, intensely, silently dramatic, waiting but the touch of the wizard wand to break out into reality, life and conflict. As such too much tribute cannot be paid to it, for it is a frightfully real presentment of all the baser passions of humanity, in both sexes, in every gradation, raised and lashed into a demoniac carnival. So far praise must be given, but it is plain through all this, that the aspect of the artist is human, intensely, powerfully human. To paint such a crowd one must probe humanity with no scrupulous knife. Pilate is self-seeking, Mary is maternal, the weeping woman is penitent, John is a strong man, rent inside with great grief, the soldiers bear the impress of the stubborn unideality of conquest; their pride is uncompromising for are they not the overcomers? It would have been easy to have made Mary a Madonna and John an evangelist but the artist has chosen to make Mary a mother and John a man. I believe this treatment to be the finer and the subtler. In a moment such as when Pilate said to the Jews, Behold the man, it would be a pious error but indubitably, an error to show Mary as the ancestress of the devout, rapt madonnas of our churches. The depicting of these two figures in such a way in a sacred picture, is in itself a token of the highest genius. If there is to be anything superhuman in the picture, anything above and beyond the heart of man, it will appear in Christ. But no matter how you view Christ, there is no trace of that in his aspect. There is nothing divine in his look, there is nothing superhuman. This is no defect of hand on the part of the artist, his skill would have accomplished anything. It was his voluntary position. Van Ruith painted a picture some years ago of Christ and the traders in the temple. His intention was to produce elevated reprimand and divine chastisement, his hand failed him and the result was a weak flogger and a mixture of loving kindness and repose, wholly incompatible with the incident. Munkacsy on the contrary would never be under the power of his brush, but his view of the event is humanistic. Consequently his work is drama. Had he chosen to paint Christ as the Incarnate Son of God, redeeming his creatures of his own admirable will, through insult and hate, it would not have been drama, it would have been Divine Law, for drama deals with man. As it is from the artist's conception, it is powerful drama, the drama of the thrice told revolt of humanity against a great teacher.

The face of Christ is a superb study of endurance, passion, I use the word in its proper sense, and dauntless will. It is plain that no thought of the crowd obtrudes itself on his mind. He seems to have nothing in common with them, save his features which are racial. The mouth is concealed by a brown mustache, the chin and up to the ears overgrown with an untrimmed but moderate beard of the same colour. The forehead is low and projects somewhat on the eyebrows. The nose is slightly Jewish but almost aquiline, the nostrils thin and sensitive. The eyes are of a pale blue colour, if of any, and as the face is turned to the light, they are lifted half under the brows, the only true position for intense agony. They are keen, but not large, and seem to pierce the air, half in inspiration, half in suffering. The whole face is of an ascetic, inspired, whole souled, wonderfully passionate man. It is Christ, as the Man of Sorrows, his raiment red as of them that tread in the winepress. It is literally Behold the Man.

It is this treatment of the theme that has led me to appraise it as a drama. It is grand, noble tragic but it makes the founder of Christianity, no more than a great social and religious reformer, a personality, of mingled majesty and power, a protagonist of a world-drama. No objections will be lodged against it on that score by the public, whose general attitude when they advert to the subject at all, is that of the painter, only less grand and less interested. Munkacsy's conception is as much greater than theirs, as an average artist is greater than an average greengrocer, but it is of the same kind, it is, to pervert Wagner, the attitude of the folk. Belief in the divinity of Christ is not a salient feature of secular Christendom. But occasional sympathy with the eternal conflict of truth and error, of right and wrong, as exemplified in the drama at Golgotha, is not beyond its approval.

JAJ
Sept. 1899.

DRAMA AND LIFE

ALTHOUGH THE RELATIONS between drama and life are, and must be of the most vital character, in the history of drama itself these do not seem to have been at all times, consistently in view. The earliest and best known drama, this side of the Caucasus, is that of Greece. I do not propose to attempt anything in the nature of a historical survey but cannot pass it by. Greek drama arose out of the cult of Dionysos, who, god of fruitage, joyfulness and earliest art, offered in his life-story a practical groundplan for the erection of a tragic and a comic theatre. In speaking of Greek drama it must be borne in mind that its rise dominated its form. The conditions of the Attic stage suggested a syllabus of greenroom proprieties and cautions to authors, which in after ages were foolishly set up as the canons of dramatic art, in all lands. Thus the Greeks handed down a code of laws which their descendants with purblind wisdom forthwith advanced to the dignity of inspired pronouncements. Beyond this, I say nothing. It may be a vulgarism, but it is literal truth to say that Greek drama is played out. For good or for bad it has done its work, which, if wrought in gold, was not upon lasting pillars. Its revival is not of dramatic but of pedagogic significance. Even in its own camp it has been superseded. When it had thriven over long in hieratic custody and in ceremonial form, it began to pall on the Aryan genius. A reaction ensued, as was inevitable; and as the classical drama had been born of religion, its follower arose out of a movement in literature. In this reaction England played an important part, for it was the power of the Shakespearean clique that dealt the deathblow to the already dying drama. Shakespeare was before all else a literary artist; humour, eloquence, a gift of seraphic music, theatrical instincts—he had a rich dower of these. The work, to which he gave such splendid impulse, was of a higher nature than that which it followed. It was far from mere drama, it was literature in dialogue. Here I must draw a line of demarcation between literature and drama.

Human society is the embodiment of changeless laws which the whimsicalities and circumstances of men and women involve and overwrap. The realm of literature is the realm of these accidental manners and humours—a spacious realm; and the true literary artist concerns himself mainly with them. Drama has to do with the underlying laws first, in all their nakedness and divine severity, and only secondarily with the motley agents who bear them out. When so much is recognised an advance has been made to a more rational and true appreciation of dramatic art. Unless some such distinction be made the result is chaos. Lyricism parades as poetic drama, psychological conversation as literary drama, and traditional farce moves over the boards with the label of comedy affixed to it.

Both of these dramas having done their work as prologues to the swelling act, they may be relegated to the department of literary curios. It is futile to say that there is no new drama or to contend that its proclamation is a huge boom [*sic*]. Space is valuable and I cannot combat these assertions. However it is to me day-clear that dramatic drama must outlive its elders, whose life is only eked by the most dexterous management and the carefullest husbanding. Over this New School some hard hits have been given and taken. The public is slow to seize truth, and its leaders quick to miscal [*sic*] it. Many, whose palates have grown accustomed to the old food, cry out peevishly against a change of diet. To these use and want is the seventh heaven. Loud are their praises of the bland blatancy of Corneille, the starchglaze of Trapassi's godliness, the Pumblechookian woodenness of Calderon. Their infantile plot juggling sets them agape, so superfine it is. Such critics are not to be taken seriously but they are droll figures! It is of course patently true that the "new" school masters them on their own ground. Compare the skill of Haddon Chambers and Douglas Jerrold, of Sudermann and Lessing. The "new" school in this branch of its art is superior. This superiority is only natural, as it accompanies work of immeasurably higher calibre. Even the least part of Wagner—his music—is beyond Bellini. Spite of the outcry of these lovers of the past, the masons are building for Drama, an ampler and loftier home, where there shall be light for gloom, and wide porches for drawbridge and keep.

Let me explain a little as to this great visitant. By drama I understand the interplay of passions to portray truth; drama is strife, evolution, movement in whatever way unfolded; it exists, before it takes form, independently; it is conditioned but not controlled by its scene. It might be said fantastically that as soon as men and women began life in the world there was above them and about them, a spirit, of which they were dimly conscious, which they would have had sojourn in their midst in deeper intimacy and for whose truth they became seekers in after times, longing to lay hands upon it. For this spirit is as the roaming air, little susceptible of change, and never left their vision, shall never leave it, till the firmament is as a scroll rolled away. At times it would seem that the spirit had taken up his abode in this or that form—but on a sudden he is misused, he is gone and the abode is left idle. He is, one might guess, somewhat of an elfish nature, a nixie, a very Ariel. So we must distinguish him and his house. An idylic [sic] portrait, or an environment of haystacks does not constitute a pastoral play, no more than rhodomontade and sermonising build up a tragedy. Neither quiescence nor vulgarity shadow forth drama. However subdued the tone of passions may be, however ordered the action or commonplace the diction, if a play or a work of music or a picture presents the everlasting hopes, desires and hates of us, or deals with a symbolic presentment of our widely related nature, albeit a phase of that nature, then it is drama. I shall not speak here of its many forms. In every form that was not fit for it, it made an outburst, as when the first sculptor separated the feet. Morality, mystery, ballet, pantomime, opera, all these it speedily ran through and discarded. Its proper form "the drama" is yet intact. "There are many candles on the high altar, though one fall."

Whatever form it takes must not be superimposed or conventional. In literature we allow conventions, for literature is a comparatively low form of art. Literature is kept alive by tonics, it flourishes through conventions in all human relations, in all actuality. Drama will be for the future at war with convention, if it is to realise itself truly. If you have a clear thought of the body of drama, it will be manifest what raiment befits it. Drama of so wholehearted and admirable a nature cannot but draw all hearts from the spectacular and the theatrical, its note being truth and freedom in every aspect of it. It may be asked what are we to do, in the words of Tolstoï. First, clear our minds of cant and alter the falsehoods to which we have lent our support. Let us criticise in the manner of free people, as a free race, recking little of ferula and formula. The Folk is, I believe, able to do so much. Securus judicat orbis terrarum, is not too high a motto for all human artwork. Let us not overbear the weak, let us treat with a tolerant smile the state pronouncements of those matchless serio-comics—the "litterateurs" [sic]. If a sanity rules the mind of the dramatic world there will be accepted what is now the faith of the few, then will be past dispute written up the respective grades of Macbeth and The Master Builder. The sententious critic of the thirtieth century may well say of them—Between him and these there is a great gulf fixed.

There are some weighty truths which we cannot overpass, in the relations between drama and the artist. Drama is essentially a communal art and of widespread domain. The drama—its fittest vehicle almost presupposes an audience, drawn from all classes. In an art-loving and art-producing society the drama would naturally take up its position at the head of all artistic institutions. Drama is moreover of so unswayed, so unchallengeable a nature that in its highest forms it all but transcends criticism. It is hardly possible to criticise The Wild Duck, for instance; one can only brood upon it as upon a personal woe. Indeed in the case of all Ibsen's later work dramatic criticism, properly so called, verges on impertinence. In every other art personality, mannerism of touch, local sense, are held as adornments, as additional charms. But here the artist forgoes his very self and stands a mediator in awful truth before the veiled face of God.

If you ask me what occasions drama or what is the necessity for it at all, I answer Necessity. It is mere animal instinct applied to the mind. Apart from his world-old desire to get beyond the flaming ramparts, man has a further longing to become a maker and a moulder. That is the necessity of all art. Drama is again the least dependent of all arts on its material. If the supply of mouldable earth or stone gives out, sculpture becomes a memory, if the yield of vegetable pigments ceases, the pictorial art ceases. But whether there be marble or paints, there is always the artstuff for drama. I believe further that drama arises spontaneously out of life and is coeval with it. Every race has made its own myths and it is in these that early drama often finds an outlet. The author of Parsifal has recognised this and hence his work is solid as rock. When the mythus passes over the borderline and invades the temple of worship, the possibilities of its drama have lessened considerably. Even then it struggles back to its rightful place, much to the discomfort of the stodgy congregation.

As men differ as to the rise, so do they as to the aims of drama. It is in most cases claimed by the votaries of the antique school that the drama should have special ethical aims, to use their stock phrase, that it should instruct, elevate, and amuse. Here is yet another gyve that the jailers have bestowed. I do not say that drama may not fulfil any or all of these functions, but I deny that it is essential that it should fulfil them. Art, elevated into the overhigh sphere of religion, generally loses its true soul in stagnant quietism. As to the lower form of this dogma it is surely funny. This polite request to the dramatist to please point a moral, to rival Cyrano, in iterating through each act "A la fin de l'envoi je touche" is amazing. Bred as it is of an amiable-parochial disposition we can but waive it. Mr Beoerly sacked with strychnine, or M Coupeau in the horrors are nothing short of piteous in a surplice and dalmatic apiece.

However this absurdity is eating itself fast, like the tiger of story, tail first.

A yet more insidious claim is the claim for beauty. As conceived by the claimants beauty is as often anaemic spirituality as hardy animalism. Then, chiefly because beauty is to men an arbitrary quality and often lies no deeper than form, to pin drama to dealing with it, would be hazardous. Beauty is the swerga of the aesthete; but truth has a more ascertainable and a more real dominion. Art is true to itself when it deals with truth. Should such an untoward event as a universal reformation take place on earth, truth would be the very threshold of the house beautiful.

I have just one other claim to discuss, even at the risk of exhausting your patience. I quote from Mr Beerbohm Tree. "In these days when faith is tinged with philosophic doubt, I believe it is the function of art to give us light rather than darkness. It should not point to our relationship with monkeys but rather remind us of our affinity with the angels." In this statement there is a fair element of truth which however requires qualification. Mr Tree contends that men and women will always look to art as the glass wherein they may see themselves idealised. Rather I should think that men and women seldom think gravely on their own impulses towards art. The fetters of convention bind them too strongly. But after all art cannot be governed by the insincerity of the compact majority but rather by those eternal conditions, says Mr Tree, which have governed it from the first. I admit this as irrefutable truth. But it were well we had in mind that those eternal conditions are not the conditions of modern communities. Art is marred by such mistaken insistence on its religious, its moral, its beautiful, its idealising tendencies. A single Rembrandt is worth a gallery full of Van Dycks. And it is this doctrine of idealism in art which has in notable instances disfigured manful endeavour, and has also fostered a babyish instinct to dive under blankets at the mention of the bogey of realism. Hence the public disowns Tragedy, unless she rattles her dagger and goblet, abhors Romance which is not amenable to the laws of prosody, and deems it a sad defect in art if, from the outpoured blood of haplẹss heroism, there does not at once spring up a growth of sorrowful blossoms. As in the very madness and frenzy of this attitude, people want the drama to befool them, Purveyor supplies plutocrat with a parody of life which the latter digests medicinally in a darkened theatre, the stage literally battening on the mental offal of its patrons.

Now if these views are effete what will serve the purpose? Shall we put life—real life—on the stage? No, says the Philistine chorus, for it will not draw. What a blend of thwarted sight and smug commercialism. Parnassus and the city Bank divide the souls of the pedlars. Life indeed nowadays is often a sad bore. Many feel like the Frenchman that they have been born too late in a world too old, and their wanhope and nerveless unheroism point on ever sternly to a last nothing, a vast futility and meanwhile—a bearing of fardels. Epic savagery is rendered impossible by vigilant policing, chivalry has been killed by the fashion oracles of the boulevardes. There is no clank of mail, no halo about gallantry, no hat-sweeping, no roystering! The traditions of romance are upheld only in Bohemia. Still I think out of the dreary sameness of existence, a measure of dramatic life may be drawn. Even the most commonplace, the deadest among the living, may play a part in a great drama. It is a sinful foolishness to sigh back for the good old times, to feed the hunger of us with the cold stones they afford. Life we must accept as we see it before our eyes, men and women as we meet them in the real world, not as we apprehend them in the world of faery. The great human comedy in which each has share, gives limitless scope to the true artist, today as yesterday and as in years gone. The forms of things, as the earth's crust, are changed. The timbers of the ships of Tarshish are falling asunder or eaten by the wanton sea; time has broken into the fastnesses of the mighty; the gardens of Armida are become as treeless wilds. But the deathless passions, the human verities which so found expression then, are indeed deathless, in the heroic cycle, or in the scientific age. Lohengrin, the drama of which unfolds itself in a scene of seclusion, amid half-lights, is not an Antwerp legend but a world drama. Ghosts, the action of which passes in a common parlour, is of universal import—a deepset branch on the tree, Igdrasil [*sic*], whose roots are struck in earth, but through whose higher leafage the stars of heaven are glowing and astir. It may be that many have nothing to do with such fable, or think that their wonted fare is all that is of need to them. But as we stand on the mountains today, looking before and after, pining for what is not, scarcely discerning afar the patches of open sky; when the spurs threaten, and the track is grown with briers, what does it avail that into our hands we have given us a clouded cane for an alpenstock, or that we have dainty silks to shield us against the eager, upland wind? The sooner we understand our true position, the better; and the sooner then will we be up and doing on our way. In the meantime, art, and chiefly drama, may help us to make our resting places with a greater insight and a greater foresight, that the stones of them may be bravely builded, and the windows goodly and fair. ". . . what will you do in our Society, Miss Hessel?" asked Rörlund—"I will let in fresh air, Pastor."—answered Lona.

Jas. A. Joyce
January.10.1900.

IBSEN'S NEW DRAMA

TWENTY YEARS HAVE passed since Henrik Ibsen wrote *A Doll's House,* thereby almost marking an epoch in the history of drama. During those years his name has gone abroad through the length and breadth of two continents, and has provoked more discussion and criticism than that of any other living man. He has been upheld as a religious reformer, a social reformer, a Semitic lover of righteousness, and as a great dramatist. He has been rigorously denounced as a meddlesome intruder, a defective artist, an incomprehensible mystic, and, in the eloquent words of a certain English critic, "a muck-ferreting dog." Through the perplexities of such diverse criticism, the great genius of the man is day by day coming out as a hero comes out amid the earthly trials. The dissonant cries are fainter and more distant, the random praises are rising in steadier and more choral chaunt. Even to the uninterested bystander it must seem significant that the interest attached to this Norwegian has never flagged for over a quarter of a century. It may be questioned whether any man has held so firm an empire over the thinking world in modern times. Not Rousseau; not Emerson; not Carlyle; not any of those giants of whom almost all have passed out of human ken. Ibsen's power over two generations has been enhanced by his own reticence. Seldom, if at all, has he condescended to join battle with his enemies. It would appear as if the storm of fierce debate rarely broke in upon his wonderful calm. The conflicting voices have not influenced his work in the very smallest degree. His output of dramas has been regulated by the utmost order, by a clockwork routine, seldom found in the case of genius. Only once he answered his assailants after

35

their violent attack on *Ghosts*. But from *The Wild Duck* to *John Gabriel Borkman,* his dramas have appeared almost mechanically at intervals of two years. One is apt to overlook the sustained energy which such a plan of campaign demands; but even surprise at this must give way to admiration at the gradual, irresistible advance of this extraordinary man. Eleven plays, all dealing with modern life, have been published. Here is the list: *A Doll's House, Ghosts, An Enemy of the People, The Wild Duck, Rosmersholm, The Lady from the Sea, Hedda Gabler, The Master Builder, Little Eyolf, John Gabriel Borkman,* and lastly—his new drama, published at Copenhagen, 19 December 1899—*When We Dead Awaken*. This play is already in process of translation into almost a dozen different languages—a fact which speaks volumes for the power of its author. The drama is written in prose, and is in three acts.

To begin an account of a play of Ibsen's is surely no easy matter. The subject is, in one way, so confined, and, in another way, so vast. It is safe to predict that nine-tenths of the notices of this play will open in some such way as the following: "Arnold Rubek and his wife, Maja, have been married for four years, at the beginning of the play. Their union is, however, unhappy. Each is discontented with the other." So far as this goes, it is unimpeachable; but then it does not go very far. It does not convey even the most shadowy notion of the relations between Professor Rubek and his wife. It is a bald, clerkly version of countless, indefinable complexities. It is as though the history of a tragic life were to be written down rudely in two columns, one for the pros and the other for the cons. It is only saying what is literally true, to say that, in the three acts of the drama, there has been stated all that is essential to the drama. There is from first to last hardly a superfluous word or phrase. Therefore, the play itself expresses its own ideas as briefly and as concisely as they can be expressed in the dramatic form. It is manifest, then, that a notice cannot give an adequate notion of the drama. This is not the case with the common lot of plays, to which the fullest justice may be meted out in a very limited number of lines. They are for the most part reheated dishes—unoriginal compositions, cheerfully owlish as to heroic insight, living only in their own candid claptrap—in a word, stagey. The most perfunctory curtness is their fittest meed. But in dealing with the work of a man like Ibsen, the task set the reviewer is truly great enough to sink all his courage. All he can hope to do is to link some of the more salient points together in such a way as to suggest rather than to indicate, the intricacies of the plot. Ibsen has attained ere this to such mastery over his art that, with apparently easy dialogue, he presents his men and women passing through different soul-crises. His analytic method is thus made use of to the fullest extent, and into the comparatively short space of two days the life in life of all his characters is compressed. For instance, though we only see Solness during one night and up to the following evening, we have in reality watched with bated breath the whole course of his life up to the moment when Hilda Wangel enters his house. So in the play under consideration, when we see Professor Rubek first, he is sitting in a garden chair, reading his morning paper, but by degrees the whole scroll of his life is unrolled before us, and we have the pleasure not of hearing it read out to us, but of reading it for ourselves, piecing the various parts, and going closer to see wherever the writing on the parchment is fainter or less legible.

As I have said, when the play opens, Professor Rubek is sitting in the gardens of a hotel, eating, or rather having finished, his breakfast. In another chair, close beside him, is sitting Maja Rubek, the Professor's wife. The scene is in Norway, a popular health resort near the sea. Through the trees can be seen the town harbour, and the fjord, with steamers plying over it, as it stretches past headland and river-isle out to the sea. Rubek is a famous sculptor, of middle age, and Maja, a woman still young, whose bright eyes have just a shade of sadness in them. These two continue reading their respective papers quietly in the peace of the morning. All looks so idyllic to the careless eye. The lady breaks the silence in a weary, petulant manner by complaining of the deep peace that reigns about them. Arnold lays down his paper with mild expostulation. Then they begin to converse of this thing and that; first of the silence, then of the place and the people, of the railway stations through which they passed the previous night, with their sleepy porters and aimlessly shifting lanterns. From this they proceed to talk of the changes in the people, and of all that has grown up since they were married. Then it is but a little further to the main trouble. In speaking of their married life it speedily appears that the inner view of their relations is hardly as ideal as the outward view might lead one to expect. The depths of these two people are being slowly stirred up. The leaven of prospective drama is gradually discerned working amid the *fin-de-siècle* scene. The lady seems a difficult little person. She complains of the idle promises with which her husband had fed her aspirations.

MAJA You said you would take me up to a high mountain and
    show me all the glory of the world.
RUBEK (*with a slight start*). Did I promise you that, too?

In short, there is something untrue lying at the root of their union. Meanwhile the guests of the hotel, who are taking the baths, pass out of the hotel porch on the right, chatting and laughing men and women. They are informally marshalled by the inspector of the baths. This person is an unmistakable type of the conventional official. He salutes Mr and Mrs Rubek, enquiring how they slept. Rubek asks him if any of the guests take their baths by night, as he has seen a white figure moving in the park during the night. Maja scouts the notion, but the inspector says that there is a strange lady, who has rented the pavilion which is to the left, and who is staying there, with one attendant—a Sister of Mercy. As they are talking, the strange lady and her companion pass slowly through the park and enter the pavilion. The incident appears to affect Rubek, and Maja's curiosity is aroused.

MAJA (*a little hurt and jarred*). Perhaps this lady has been one of
    your models, Rubek? Search your memory.
RUBEK (*looks cuttingly at her*). Model?
MAJA (*with a provoking smile*). In your younger days, I mean.
    You are said to have had such innumerable models—long
    ago, of course.

RUBEK (*in the same tone*). Oh, no, little Frau Maja. I have in reality had only one single model. One and one only for everything I have done.

While this misunderstanding is finding outlet in the foregoing conversation, the inspector, all at once, takes fright at some person who is approaching. He attempts to escape into the hotel, but the high-pitched voice of the person who is approaching arrests him.

ULFHEIM'S voice (*heard outside*). Stop a moment, man. Devil take it all, can't you stop? Why do you always scuttle away from me?

With these words, uttered in strident tones, the second chief actor enters on the scene. He is described as a great bear-killer, thin, tall, of uncertain age, and muscular. He is accompanied by his servant, Lars, and a couple of sporting dogs. Lars does not speak a single word in the play. Ulfheim at present dismisses him with a kick, and approaches Mr and Mrs Rubek. He falls into conversation with them, for Rubek is known to him as the celebrated sculptor. On sculpture this savage hunter offers some original remarks.

ULFHEIM. . . . We both work in a hard material, madam—both your husband and I. He struggles with his marble blocks, I daresay; and I struggle with tense and quivering bear-sinews. And we both of us win the fight in the end—subdue and master our material. We don't give in until we have got the better of it, though it fight never so hard.

RUBEK (*deep in thought*). There's a great deal of truth in what you say.

This eccentric creature, perhaps by the force of his own eccentricity, has begun to weave a spell of enchantment about Maja. Each word that he utters tends to wrap the web of his personality still closer about her. The black dress of the Sister of Mercy causes him to grin sardonically. He speaks calmly of all his near friends, whom he has dispatched out of the world.

MAJA. And what did you do for your nearest friends?
ULFHEIM. Shot them, of course.
RUBEK (*looking at him*). Shot them?
MAJA (*moving her chair back*). Shot them dead?
ULFHEIM (*nods*). I never miss, madam

However, it turns out that by his nearest friends he means his dogs, and the minds of his hearers are put somewhat more at ease. During their conversation the Sister of Mercy has prepared a slight repast for her mistress at one of the tables outside the pavilion. The unsustaining qualities of the food excite Ulfheim's merriment. He speaks with a lofty disparagement of such effeminate diet. He is a realist in his appetite.

ULFHEIM (*rising*). Spoken like a woman of spirit, madam. Come with me, then! They [his dogs] swallow whole, great, thumping meat-bones—gulp them up and then gulp them down again. Oh, it's a regular treat to see them!

On such half-gruesome, half-comic invitation Maja goes out with him, leaving her husband in the company of the strange lady who enters from the pavilion. Almost simultaneously the Professor and the lady recognise each other. The lady has served Rubek as model for the central figure in his famous masterpiece, "The Resurrection Day." Having done her work for him, she had fled in an unaccountable manner, leaving no traces behind her. Rubek and she drift into familiar conversation. She asks him who is the lady who has just gone out. He answers, with some hesitation, that she is his wife. Then he asks if she is married. She replies that she is married. He asks her where her husband is at present.

RUBEK. And where is he now?
IRENE. Oh, in a churchyard somewhere or other, with a fine, handsome monument over him; and with a bullet rattling in his skull.
RUBEK. Did he kill himself?
IRENE. Yes, he was good enough to take that off my hands.

RUBEK. Do you not lament his loss, Irene?

IRENE (*not understanding*). Lament? What loss?

RUBEK. Why, the loss of Herr von Satow, of course.

IRENE. His name was not Satow.

RUBEK. Was it not?

IRENE. My second husband is called Satow. He is a Russian.

RUBEK. And where is he?

IRENE. Far away in the Ural Mountains. Among all his gold-mines.

RUBEK. So he lives there?

IRENE (*shrugging her shoulders*). Lives? Lives? In reality I have killed him.

RUBEK (*starts*). Killed——!

IRENE. Killed him with a fine sharp dagger which I always have with me in bed—

Rubek begins to understand that there is some meaning hidden beneath these strange words. He begins to think seriously on himself, his art, and on her, passing in review the course of his life since the creation of his masterpiece, "The Resurrection Day." He sees that he has not fulfilled the promise of that work, and comes to realise that there is something lacking in his life. He asks Irene how she has lived since they last saw each other. Irene's answer to this query is of great importance, for it strikes the keynote of the entire play.

IRENE (*rises slowly from her chair and says quiveringly*). I was dead for many years. They came and bound me—lacing my arms together at my back. Then they lowered me into a grave-vault, with iron bars before the loophole. And with padded walls, so that no one on the earth above could hear the grave-shrieks.

In Irene's allusion to her position as model for the great picture, Ibsen gives further proof of his extraordinary knowledge of women. No other man could have so subtly expressed the nature of the relations between the sculptor and his model, had he even dreamt of them.

IRENE. I exposed myself wholly and unreservedly to your gaze [*more softly*] and never once did you touch me. . . .

★

RUBEK (*looks impressively at her*). I was an artist, Irene.
IRENE (*darkly*). That is just it. That is just it.

Thinking deeper and deeper on himself and on his former attitude towards this woman, it strikes him yet more forcibly that there are great gulfs set between his art and his life, and that even in his art his skill and genius are far from perfect. Since Irene left him he has done nothing but paint portrait busts of townsfolk. Finally, some kind of resolution is enkindled in him, a resolution to repair his botching, for he does not altogether despair of that. There is just a reminder of the will-glorification of *Brand* in the lines that follow.

RUBEK (*struggling with himself uncertainly*). If we could, oh, if only we could . . .
IRENE. Why can we not do what we will?

In fine, the two agree in deeming their present state insufferable. It appears plain to her that Rubek lies under a heavy obligation to her, and with their recognition of this, and the entrance of Maja, fresh from the enchantment of Ulfheim, the first act closes.

RUBEK. When did you begin to seek for me, Irene?
IRENE (*with a touch of jesting bitterness*). From the time when I realised that I had given away to you something rather indispensable. Something one ought never to part with.
RUBEK (*bowing his head*). Yes, that is bitterly true. You gave me three or four years of your youth.
IRENE. More, more than that I gave you—spendthrift as I then was.
RUBEK. Yes, you were prodigal, Irene. You gave me all your naked loveliness—
IRENE. To gaze upon—

RUBEK. And to glorify. . . .

★

IRENE. But you have forgotten the most precious gift.
RUBEK. The most precious . . . what gift was that?
IRENE. I gave you my young living soul. And that gift left me
    empty within—soulless [*looks at him with a fixed stare*]. It was
    that I died of, Arnold.

It is evident, even from this mutilated account, that the first
act is a masterly one. With no perceptible effort the drama rises,
with a methodic natural ease it develops. The trim garden of
the nineteenth-century hotel is slowly made the scene of a
gradually growing dramatic struggle. Interest has been roused
in each of the characters, sufficient to carry the mind into the
succeeding act. The situation is not stupidly explained, but the
action has set in, and at the close the play has reached a definite
stage of progression.

The second act takes place close to a sanatorium on the
mountains. A cascade leaps from a rock and flows in steady
stream to the right. On the bank some children are playing,
laughing and shouting. The time is evening. Rubek is
discovered lying on a mound to the left. Maja enters shortly,
equipped for hill-climbing. Helping herself with her stick
across the stream, she calls out to Rubek and approaches him.
He asks how she and her companion are amusing themselves,
and questions her as to their hunting. An exquisitely humorous
touch enlivens their talk. Rubek asks if they intend hunting
the bear near the surrounding locality. She replies with a
grand superiority.

MAJA. You don't suppose that bears are to be found in the
    naked mountains, do you?

The next topic is the uncouth Ulfheim. Maja admires him
because he is so ugly—then turns abruptly to her husband
saying, pensively, that he also is ugly. The accused pleads
his age.

RUBEK (*shrugging his shoulders*). One grows old. One grows old, Frau Maja!

This semi-serious banter leads them on to graver matters. Maja lies at length in the soft heather, and rails gently at the Professor. For the mysteries and claims of art she has a somewhat comical disregard.

MAJA (*with a somewhat scornful laugh*). Yet, you are always, always an artist.

and again—

MAJA. . . . Your tendency is to keep yourself to yourself and—think your own thoughts. And, of course, I can't talk properly to you about your affairs. I know nothing about Art and that sort of thing. [*With an impatient gesture.*] And care very little either, for that matter.

She rallies him on the subject of the strange lady, and hints maliciously at the understanding between them. Rubek says that he was only an artist and that she was the source of his inspiration. He confesses that the five years of his married life have been years of intellectual famine for him. He has viewed in their true light his own feelings towards his art.

RUBEK (*smiling*). But that was not precisely what I had in my mind.
MAJA. What then?
RUBEK (*again serious*). It was this—that all the talk about the artist's vocation and the artist's mission, and so forth, began to strike me as being very empty and hollow and meaningless at bottom.
MAJA. Then what would you put in its place?
RUBEK. Life, Maja.

The all-important question of their mutual happiness is touched upon, and after a brisk discussion a tacit agreement to

separate is effected. When matters are in this happy condition
Irene is descried coming across the heath. She is surrounded
by the sportive children and stays awhile among them. Maja
jumps up from the grass and goes to her, saying, enigmatically,
that her husband requires assistance to "open a precious casket."
Irene bows and goes towards Rubek, and Maja goes joyfully
to seek her hunter. The interview which follows is certainly
remarkable, even from a stagey point of view. It constitutes,
practically, the substance of the second act, and is of absorbing
interest. At the same time it must be added that such a scene
would tax the powers of the mimes producing it. Nothing
short of a complete realisation of the two *rôles* would represent
the complex ideas involved in the conversation. When we
reflect how few stage artists would have either the intelligence
to attempt it or the powers to execute it, we behold a pitiful
revelation.

In the interview of these two people on the heath, the whole
tenors of their lives are outlined with bold steady strokes. From
the first exchange of introductory words each phrase tells a
chapter of experiences. Irene alludes to the dark shadow of
the Sister of Mercy which follows her everywhere, as the
shadow of Arnold's unquiet conscience follows him. When
he has half-involuntarily confessed so much, one of the great
barriers between them is broken down. Their trust in each
other is, to some extent, renewed, and they revert to their
past acquaintance. Irene speaks openly of her feelings, of her
hate for the sculptor.

IRENE (*again vehemently*). Yes, for you—for the artist who had
so lightly and carelessly taken a warm-blooded body, a young
human life, and worn the soul out of it—because you needed
it for a work of art.

Rubek's transgression has indeed been great. Not merely has
he possessed himself of her soul, but he has withheld from its
rightful throne the child of her soul. By her child Irene means
the statue. To her it seems that this statue is, in a very true and
very real sense, born of her. Each day as she saw it grow to its

full growth under the hand of the skilful moulder, her inner sense of motherhood for it, of right over it, of love towards it, had become stronger and more confirmed.

IRENE (*changing to a tone full of warmth and feeling*). But that statue in the wet, living clay, that I loved—as it rose up, a vital human creature out of these raw, shapeless masses—for that was our creation, our child. Mine and yours.

It is, in reality, because of her strong feelings that she has kept aloof from Rubek for five years. But when she hears now of what he has done to the child—her child—all her powerful nature rises up against him in resentment. Rubek, in a mental agony, endeavours to explain, while she listens like a tigress whose cub has been wrested from her by a thief.

RUBEK. I was young then—with no experience of life. The Resurrection, I thought, would be most beautifully and exquisitely figured as a young unsullied woman—with none of a life's experience—awakening to light and glory without having to put away from her anything ugly and impure.

With larger experience of life he has found it necessary to alter his ideal somewhat, he has made her child no longer a principal, but an intermediary figure. Rubek, turning towards her, sees her just about to stab him. In a fever of terror and thought he rushes into his own defence, pleading madly for the errors he has done. It seems to Irene that he is endeavouring to render his sin poetical, that he is penitent but in a luxury of dolour. The thought that she has given up herself, her whole life, at the bidding of his false art, rankles in her heart with a terrible persistence. She cries out against herself, not loudly, but in deep sorrow.

IRENE (*with apparent self-control*). I should have borne children into the world—many children—real children—not such children as are hidden away in grave-vaults. That was my vocation. I ought never to have served you—poet.

Rubek, in poetic absorption, has no reply, he is musing on the old, happy days. Their dead joys solace him. But Irene is thinking of a certain phrase of his which he had spoken unwittingly. He had declared that he owed her thanks for her assistance in his work. This has been, he had said, a truly blessed *episode* in my life. Rubek's tortured mind cannot bear any more reproaches, too many are heaped upon it already. He begins throwing flowers on the stream, as they used in those bygone days on the lake of Taunitz. He recalls to her the time when they made a boat of leaves, and yoked a white swan to it, in imitation of the boat of Lohengrin. Even here in their sport there lies a hidden meaning.

IRENE. You said I was the swan that drew your boat.
RUBEK. Did I say so? Yes, I daresay I did [*absorbed in the game*].
    Just see how the sea-gulls are swimming down the stream!
IRENE (*laughing*). And all your ships have run ashore.
RUBEK (*throwing more leaves into the brook*). I have ships enough
    in reserve.

While they are playing aimlessly, in a kind of childish despair, Ulfheim and Maja appear across the heath. These two are going to seek adventures on the high tablelands. Maja sings out to her husband a little song which she has composed in her joyful mood. With a sardonic laugh Ulfheim bids Rubek good-night and disappears with his companion up the mountain. All at once Irene and Rubek leap to the same thought. But at that moment the gloomy figure of the Sister of Mercy is seen in the twilight, with her leaden eyes looking at them both. Irene breaks from him, but promises to meet him that night on the heath.

RUBEK. And you will come, Irene?
IRENE. Yes, certainly I will come. Wait for me here.
RUBEK (*repeats dreamily*). Summer night on the upland. With
    you. With you. [*His eyes meet hers.*] Oh, Irene, that might
    have been our life. And that we have forfeited, we two.
IRENE. We see the irretrievable only when [*breaks off short*].

RUBEK (*looks inquiringly at her*). When?. . .
IRENE. When we dead awaken.

The third act takes place on a wide plateau, high up on the hills. The ground is rent with yawning clefts. Looking to the right, one sees the range of the summits half-hidden in the moving mists. On the left stands an old, dismantled hut. It is in the early morning, when the skies are the colour of pearl. The day is beginning to break. Maja and Ulfheim come down to the plateau. Their feelings are sufficiently explained by the opening words.

MAJA (*trying to tear herself loose*). Let me go! Let me go, I say!
ULFHEIM. Come, come! are you going to bite now? You're as snappish as a wolf.

When Ulfheim will not cease his annoyances, Maja threatens to run over the crest of the neighbouring ridge. Ulfheim points out that she will dash herself to pieces. He has wisely sent Lars away after the hounds, that he may be uninterrupted. Lars, he says, may be trusted not to find the dogs too soon.

MAJA (*looking angrily at him*). No, I daresay not.
ULFHEIM (*catching at her arm*). For Lars—he knows my—my methods of sport, you see.

Maja, with enforced self-possession, tells him frankly what she thinks of him. Her uncomplimentary observations please the bear-hunter very much. Maja requires all her tact to keep him in order. When she talks of going back to the hotel, he gallantly offers to carry her on his shoulders, for which suggestion he is promptly snubbed. The two are playing as a cat and a bird play. Out of their skirmish one speech of Ulfheim's rises suddenly to arrest attention, as it throws some light on his former life.

ULFHEIM (*with suppressed exasperation*). I once took a young girl—lifted her up from the mire of the streets, and carried

her in my arms. Next my heart I carried her. So I would
have borne her all through life, lest haply she should dash
her foot against a stone . . . [*With a growling laugh.*] And do
you know what I got for my reward?

MAJA. No. What did you get?

ULFHEIM (*looks at her, smiles and nods*). I got the horns! The
horns that you can see so plainly. Is not that a comical story,
madam bear-murderess?

As an exchange of confidence, Maja tells him her life in
summary—and chiefly her married life with Professor Rubek.
As a result, these two uncertain souls feel attracted to each
other, and Ulfheim states his case in the following characteristic
manner:—

ULFHEIM. Should not we two tack our poor shreds of life
together?

Maja, satisfied that in their vows there will be no promise on
his part to show her all the splendours of the earth, or to fill
her dwelling-place with art, gives a half-consent by allowing
him to carry her down the slope. As they are about to go,
Rubek and Irene, who have also spent the night on the heath,
approach the same plateau. When Ulfheim asks Rubek if he
and madame have ascended by the same pathway, Rubek
answers significantly.

RUBEK. Yes, of course [*with a glance at* MAJA]. Henceforth the
strange lady and I do not intend our ways to part.

While the musketry of their wit is at work, the elements
seem to feel that there is a mighty problem to be solved then
and there, and that a great drama is swiftly drawing to a
close. The smaller figures of Maja and Ulfheim are grown
still smaller in the dawn of the tempest. Their lots are decided
in comparative quiet, and we cease to take much interest in
them. But the other two hold our gaze, as they stand up
silently on the fjaell, engrossing central figures of boundless,

human interest. On a sudden, Ulfheim raises his hand impressively towards the heights

ULFHEIM. But don't you see that the storm is upon us? Don't you hear the blasts of wind?
RUBEK (*listening*). They sound like the prelude to the Resurrection Day. . . .

*

MAJA (*drawing* ULFHEIM *away*). Let us make haste and get down.

As he cannot take more than one person at a time, Ulfheim promises to send aid for Rubek and Irene, and, seizing Maja in his arms, clambers rapidly but warily down the path. On the desolate mountain plateau, in the growing light, the man and the woman are left together—no longer the artist and his model. And the shadow of a great change is stalking close in the morning silence. Then Irene tells Arnold that she will not go back among the men and women she has left; she will not be rescued. She tells him also, for now she may tell all, how she had been tempted to kill him in frenzy when he spoke of their connection as an episode of his life.

RUBEK (*darkly*). And why did you hold your hand?
IRENE. Because it flashed upon me with a sudden horror that you were dead already—long ago.

But, says Rubek, our love is not dead in us, it is active, fervent and strong.

IRENE. The love that belongs to the life of earth—the beautiful, miraculous life of earth—the inscrutable life of earth—that is dead in both of us.

There are, moreover, the difficulties of their former lives. Even here, at the sublimest part of his play, Ibsen is master of himself and his facts. His genius as an artist faces all, shirks nothing. At the close of *The Master Builder,* the greatest touch of all was the horrifying exclamation of one without, "O! the head is all crushed in." A lesser artist would have cast a spiritual glamour over the tragedy of Bygmester Solness. In like manner here Irene objects that she has exposed herself as a nude before the vulgar gaze, that Society has cast her out, that all is too late. But Rubek cares for such considerations no more. He flings them all to the wind and decides.

RUBEK (*throwing his arms violently around her*). Then let two of the dead—us two—for once live life to its uttermost, before we go down to our graves again.

IRENE (*with a shriek*). Arnold!

RUBEK. But not here in the half-darkness. Not here with this hideous dank shroud flapping around us!

IRENE (*carried away by passion*). No, no—up in the light and in all the glittering glory! Up to the Peak of Promise!

RUBEK. There we will hold our marriage-feast, Irene—oh! my beloved!

IRENE (*proudly*). The sun may freely look on us, Arnold.

RUBEK. All the powers of light may freely look on us—and all the powers of darkness too [*seizes her hand*]—will you then follow me, oh my grace-given bride!

IRENE (*as though transfigured*). I follow you, freely and gladly, my lord and master!

RUBEK (*drawing her along with him*). We must first pass through the mists, Irene, and then—

IRENE. Yes, through all the mists, and then right up to the summit of the tower that shines in the sunrise.

> [*The mist-clouds close in over the scene.* RUBEK *and* IRENE, *hand in hand, climb up over the snowfield to the right and soon disappear among the lower clouds. Keen storm-gusts hurtle and whistle through the air.*
> [THE SISTER OF MERCY *appears upon the rubble-slope to the left. She stops and looks around silently and searchingly.*
> [MAJA *can be heard singing triumphantly far in the depths below.*

MAJA. I am free! I am free! I am free!
No more life in the prison for me!
I am free as a bird! I am free!

[*Suddenly a sound like thunder is heard from high up on the snowfield, which glides and whirls downwards with rushing speed.* RUBEK *and* IRENE *can be dimly discerned as they are whirled along with the masses of snow and buried in them.*

THE SISTER OF MERCY (*gives a shriek, stretches out her arms towards them, and cries*). Irene! [*Stands silent a moment, then makes the sign of the cross before her in the air, and says*], Pax Vobiscum!
[MAJA'S *triumphant song sounds from still further down below.*

Such is the plot, in a crude and incoherent way, of this new drama. Ibsen's plays do not depend for their interest on the action, or on the incidents. Even the characters, faultlessly drawn though they be, are not the first thing in his plays. But the naked drama—either the perception of a great truth, or the opening up of a great question, or a great conflict which is almost independent of the conflicting actors, and has been and is of far-reaching importance—this is what primarily rivets our attention. Ibsen has chosen the average lives in their uncompromising truth for the groundwork of all his later plays. He has abandoned the verse form, and has never sought to embellish his work after the conventional fashion. Even when his dramatic theme reached its zenith he has not sought to trick it out in gawds or tawdriness. How easy it would have been to have written *An Enemy of the People* on a speciously loftier level—to have replaced the *bourgeois* by the legitimate hero! Critics might then have extolled as grand what they have so often condemned as banal. But the surroundings are nothing to Ibsen. The play is the thing. By the force of his genius, and the indisputable skill which he brings to all his efforts, Ibsen has, for many years, engrossed the attention of the civilised world. Many years more, however, must pass before he will enter his kingdom in jubilation, although, as he stands to-day, all has been done on his part to ensure his own worthiness to enter therein. I do not propose here to examine into every detail of dramaturgy connected with this play, but merely to outline the characterisation.

In his characters Ibsen does not repeat himself. In this drama—the last of a long catalogue—he has drawn and differentiated with his customary skill. What a novel creation is Ulfheim! Surely the hand which has drawn him has not yet lost her cunning. Ulfheim is, I think, the newest character in the play. He is a kind of surprise-packet. It is as a result of his novelty that he seems to leap, at first mention, into bodily form. He is superbly wild, primitively impressive. His fierce eyes roll and glare as those of Yégof or Herne. As for Lars, we may dismiss him, for he never opens his mouth. The Sister of Mercy speaks only once in the play, but then with good effect. In silence she follows Irene like a retribution, a voiceless shadow with her own symbolic majesty.

Irene, too, is worthy of her place in the gallery of her compeers. Ibsen's knowledge of humanity is nowhere more obvious than in his portrayal of women. He amazes one by his painful introspection; he seems to know them better than they know themselves. Indeed, if one may say so of an eminently virile man, there is a curious admixture of the woman in his nature. His marvellous accuracy, his faint traces of femininity, his delicacy of swift touch, are perhaps attributable to this admixture. But that he knows women is an incontrovertible fact. He appears to have sounded them to almost unfathomable depths. Beside his portraits the psychological studies of Hardy and Turgénieff, or the exhaustive elaborations of Meredith, seem no more than sciolism. With a deft stroke, in a phrase, in a word, he does what costs them chapters, and does it better. Irene, then, has to face great comparison; but it must be acknowledged that she comes forth of it bravely. Although Ibsen's women are uniformly true, they, of course, present themselves in various lights.

Thus Gina Ekdal is, before all else, a comic figure, and Hedda Gabler a tragic one—if such old-world terms may be employed without incongruity. But Irene cannot be so readily classified; the very aloofness from passion, which is not separable from her, forbids classification. She interests us strangely—magnetically, because of her inner power of character. However perfect Ibsen's former creations may be, it is questionable whether any of his women reach to the depth of soul of Irene. She holds our gaze for the sheer force of her intellectual capacity. She is, moreover, an intensely spiritual creation—in the truest and widest sense of that. At times she is liable to get beyond us, to soar above us, as she does with Rubek. It will be considered by some as a blemish that she— a woman of fine spirituality—is made an artist's model, and some may even regret that such an episode mars the harmony of the drama. I cannot altogether see the force of this contention; it seems pure irrelevancy. But whatever may be thought of the fact, there is small room for complaint as to the handling of it. Ibsen treats it, as indeed he treats all things, with large insight, artistic restraint, and sympathy. He sees it steadily and whole, as from a great height, with perfect vision and an angelic dispassionateness, with the sight of one who may look on the sun with open eyes. Ibsen is different from the clever purveyor.

Maja fulfills a certain technical function in the play, apart from her individual character. Into the sustained tension she comes as a relief. Her airy freshness is as a breath of keen air. The sense of free, almost flamboyant, life, which is her chief note, counter-balances the austerity of Irene and the dulness of Rubek. Maja has practically the same effect on this play, as Hilda Wangel has on *The Master Builder*. But she does not capture our sympathy so much as Nora Helmer. She is not meant to capture it.

Rubek himself is the chief figure in this drama, and, strangely enough, the most conventional. Certainly, when contrasted with his Napoleonic predecessor, John Gabriel Borkman, he is a mere shadow. It must be borne in mind, however, that Borkman is alive, actively, energetically, restlessly alive, all through the play to the end, when he dies; whereas Arnold Rubek is dead, almost hopelessly dead, until the end, when he comes to life. Notwithstanding this, he is supremely interesting, not because of himself, but because of his dramatic significance.

Ibsen's drama, as I have said, is wholly independent of his characters. They may be bores, but the drama in which they live and move is invariably powerful. Not that Rubek is a bore by any means! He is infinitely more interesting in himself than Torvald Helmer or Tesman, both of whom possess certain strongly-marked characteristics. Arnold Rubek is, on the other hand, not intended to be a genius, as perhaps Eljert Lovborg is. Had he been a genius like Eljert he would have understood in a truer way the value of his life. But, as we are to suppose, the facts that he is devoted to his art and that he has attained to a degree of mastery in it—mastery of hand linked with limitation of thought—tell us that there may be lying dormant in him a capacity for greater life, which may be exercised when he, a dead man, shall have risen from among the dead.

The only character whom I have neglected is the inspector of the baths, and I hasten to do him tardy, but scant, justice. He is neither more nor less than the average inspector of baths. But he is that.

So much for the characterisation, which is at all times profound and interesting. But apart from the characters in the play, there are some noteworthy points in the frequent and extensive side-issues of the line of thought. The most salient of these is what seems, at first sight, nothing more than an accidental scenic feature. I allude to the environment of the drama. One cannot but observe in Ibsen's later work a tendency to get out of closed rooms. Since *Hedda Gabler* this tendency is most marked. The last act of *The Master Builder* and the last act of *John Gabriel Borkman* take place in the open air. But in this play the three acts are *al fresco*. To give heed to such details as these in the drama may be deemed ultra-Boswellian fanaticism. As a matter of fact it is what is barely due to the work of a great artist. And this feature, which is so prominent, does not seem to me altogether without its significance.

Again, there has not been lacking in the last few social dramas a fine pity for men—a note nowhere audible in the uncompromising rigour of the early eighties. Thus in the conversion of Rubek's views as to the girl-figure in his masterpiece, "The Resurrection Day," there is involved an all-embracing philosophy, a deep sympathy with the cross-purposes and contradictions of life, as they may be reconcilable with a hopeful awakening—when the manifold travail of our poor humanity may have a glorious issue. As to the drama itself, it is doubtful if any good purpose can be served by attempting to criticise it. Many things would tend to prove this. Henrik Ibsen is one of the world's great men before whom criticism can make but feeble show. Appreciation, hearkening is the only true criticism. Further, that species of criticism which calls itself dramatic criticism is a needless adjunct to his plays. When the art of a dramatist is perfect the critic is superfluous. Life is not to be criticised, but to be faced and lived. Again, if any plays demand a stage they are the plays of Ibsen. Not merely is this so because his plays have so much in common with the plays of other men that they were not written to cumber the shelves of a library, but because they are so packed with thought. At some chance expression the mind is tortured with some question, and in a flash long reaches of life are opened up in vista, yet the vision is momentary unless we stay to ponder on it. It is just to prevent excessive pondering that Ibsen requires to be acted. Finally, it is foolish to expect that a problem, which has occupied Ibsen for nearly three years, will unroll smoothly before our eyes on a first or second reading. So it is better to leave the drama to plead for itself. But this at least is clear, that in this play Ibsen has given us nearly the very best of himself. The action is neither hindered by many complexities, as in *The Pillars of Society,* nor harrowing in its simplicity, as in *Ghosts.* We have whimsicality, bordering on extravagance, in the wild Ulfheim, and subtle humour in the sly contempt which Rubek and Maja entertain for each other. But Ibsen has striven to let the drama have perfectly free action. So he has not bestowed his wonted pains on the minor characters. In many of his plays these minor characters are matchless creations. Witness Jacob Engstrand, Tönnesen, and the demonic Molvik! But in this play the minor characters are not allowed to divert our attention.

On the whole, *When We Dead Awaken* may rank with the greatest of the author's work—if, indeed, it be not the greatest.

It is described as the last of the series, which began with *A Doll's House*—a grand epilogue to its ten predecessors. Than these dramas, excellent alike in dramaturgic skill, characterisation, and supreme interest, the long roll of drama, ancient or modern, has few things better to show.

James A. Joyce.

THE DAY OF THE RABBLEMENT

No MAN, SAID the Nolan, can be a lover of the true or the good unless he abhors the multitude; and the artist, though he may employ the crowd, is very careful to isolate himself. This radical principle of artistic economy applies specially to a time of crisis, and today when the highest form of art has been just preserved by desperate sacrifices, it is strange to see the artist making terms with the rabblement. The Irish Literary Theatre is the latest movement of protest against the sterility and falsehood of the modern stage. Half a century ago the note of protest was uttered in Norway, and since then in several countries long and disheartening battles have been fought against the hosts of prejudice and misinterpretation and ridicule. What triumph there has been here and there is due to stubborn conviction, and every movement that has set out heroically has achieved a little. The Irish Literary Theatre gave out that it was the champion of progress, and proclaimed war against commercialism and vulgarity. It had partly made good its word and was expelling the old devil, when after the first encounter it surrendered to the popular will. Now, your popular devil is more dangerous than your vulgar devil. Bulk and lungs count for something, and he can gild his speech aptly. He has prevailed once more, and the Irish Literary Theatre must now be considered the property of the rabblement of the most belated race in Europe.

It will be interesting to examine here. The official organ of the movement spoke of producing European masterpieces, but the matter went no further. Such a project was absolutely necessary. The censorship is powerless in Dublin, and the directors could have produced *Ghosts* or *The Dominion of Darkness* if they chose. Nothing can be done until the forces that dictate public judgement are calmly confronted. But, of course, the directors are shy of presenting Ibsen, Tolstoy or Hauptmaun [*sic*], where even *Countess Cathleen* is pronounced vicious and damnable. Even for a technical reason this project was necessary. A nation which never advanced so far as a miracle-play affords no literary model to the artist, and he must look abroad. Earnest dramatists of the second rank, Sudermaun [*sic*], Bypruson [*sic*], and Giocosa [*sic*], can write very much better plays than the Irish Literary Theatre has staged. But, of course, the directors would not like to present such improper writers to the uncultivated, much less to the cultivated, rabblement. Accordingly, the rabblement, placid and intensely moral, is enthroned in boxes and galleries amid a hum of approval—*la bestia Trioufaute* [*sic*]—and those who think that Echegaray is "morbid," and titter coyly when Mélisande lets down her hair, are not sure but they are the trustees of every intellectual and poetic treasure.

Meanwhile, what of the artists? It is equally unsafe at present to say of Mr Yeats that he has or has not genius. In aim and form *The Wind among the Reeds* is poetry of the highest order, and *The Adoration of the Magi* (a story which one of the great Russians might have written) shows what Mr Yeats can do when he breaks with the half-gods. But an esthete has a floating will, and Mr Yeats's treacherous instinct of adaptability must be blamed for his recent association with a platform from which even self-respect should have urged him to refrain. Mr Martyn and Mr Moore are not writers of much originality. Mr Martyn, disabled as he is by an incorrigible style, has none of the fierce, hysterical power of Strindberg, whom he suggests at times; and with him one is conscious of a lack of breadth and distinction which outweighs the nobility of certain passages. Mr Moore, however, has wonderful mimetic ability, and some years ago his books might have entitled him to the place of honour among English novelists. But though *Vain Fortune* (perhaps one should add some of *Esther Waters*) is fine, original work, Mr Moore is really struggling in the backwash of that tide which has advanced from Flaubert through Jakobsen to D'Aununzio [*sic*]: for two entire eras lie between *Madame Bovary* and *Il Fuoco*. It is plain from *Celebates* [*sic*] and the latter novels that Mr Moore is beginning to draw upon his literary account, and the quest of a new impulse may explain his recent startling conversion. Converts are in the movement now, and Mr Moore and his island have been fitly admired. But however frankly Mr Moore may misquote Pater and Turgeuieff [*sic*] to defend himself, his new impulse has no kind of relation to the future of art.

In such circumstances it has become imperative to define the position. If an artist courts the favour of the multitude he cannot escape the contagion of its fetichism and deliberate self-deception, and if he joins in a popular movement he does so at his own risk. Therefore, the Irish Literary Theatre by its surrender to the trolls has cut itself adrift from the line of advancement. Until he has freed himself from the mean influences about him—sodden enthusiasm and clever insinuation and every flattering influence of vanity and low ambition—no man is an artist at all. But his true servitude is that he inherits a will broken by doubt and a soul that yields up all its hate to a caress; and the most seeming-independent are those who are the first to reassume their bonds. But Truth deals largely with us. Elsewhere there are men who are worthy to carry on the tradition of the old master who is dying in Christiania. He has already found his successor in the writer of *Michael Kramer,* and the third minister will not be wanting when his hour comes. Even now that hour may be standing by the door.

JAS. A. JOYCE
October 15th, 1901

AN IRISH POET

Review of *Poems and Ballads of William Rooney.*

THESE ARE THE verses of a writer lately dead, whom many consider the Davis of the latest national movement. They are issued from headquarters, and are preceded by two introductions wherein there is much said concerning the working man, mutual improvement, the superior person, shady musical plays, etc. They are illustrative of the national temper, and because they are so the writers of the introductions do not hesitate to claim for them the highest honours. But this claim cannot be allowed, unless it is supported by certain evidences of literary sincerity. For a man who writes a book cannot be excused by his good intentions, or by his moral character; he enters into a region where there is question of the written word, and it is well that this should be borne in mind, now that the region of literature is assailed so fiercely by the enthusiast and the doctrinaire. An examination of the poems and ballads of William Rooney does not warrant one in claiming for them any high honours. The theme is consistently national, so uncompromising, indeed, that the reader must lift an eyebrow and assure himself when he meets on page 114 the name of D'Arcy MacGee. But the treatment of the theme does not show the same admirable consistency. In "S. Patrick's Day" and in "Dromceat" one cannot but see an uninteresting imitation of Denis Florence M'Carthy and of Ferguson; even Mr T. D. Sullivan and Mr Rolleston have done something in the making of this book. But "Roilig na Riogh" [*sic*] is utterly lacking in the high distinctive virtue of "The Dead at

63

Clonmacnoise," and Mr Rolleston, who certainly is not driven along by any poetic impulse, has written a poem because the very failure of the poetic impulse pleases in an epitaph. So much can careful writing achieve, and there can be no doubt that little is achieved in these verses, because the writing is so careless, and is yet so studiously mean. For, if carelessness is carried very far, it is like to become a positive virtue, but an ordinary carelessness is nothing but a false and mean expression of a false and mean idea. Mr Rooney, indeed, is almost a master in that "style," which is neither good nor bad. In the verses of Maedhbh he writes:

> 'Mid the sheltering hills, by the spreading waters,
> They laid her down and her cairn raised
> The fiercest-hearted of Erin's daughters—
> The bravest nature that ever blazed.

Here the writer has not devised, he has merely accepted, mean expressions, and even where he has accepted a fine expression, he cannot justify his use of it. Mangan's Homeric epithet of "wine-dark" becomes in his paper a colourless and meaningless epithet, which may cover any or all of the colours of the spectrum. How differently did Mangan write when he wrote:

> Knowest thou the castle that beetles over
> The wine-dark sea!

Here a colour rises in the mind and is set firmly against the golden glow in the lines that follow. But one must not look for these things when patriotism has laid hold of the writer. He has no care then to create anything according to the art of literature, not the greatest of the arts, indeed, but at least an art with a definite tradition behind it, possessing definite forms. Instead we find in these pages a weary succession of verses, "prize" poems—the worst of all. They were written, it seems, for papers and societies week after week, and they bear witness to some desperate and weary energy. But they have no spiritual and living energy, because they come from one in whom the spirit is in a manner dead, or at least in its own hell, a weary and foolish spirit, speaking of redemption and revenge, blaspheming against tyrants, and going forth, full of tears and curses, upon its infernal labours. Religion and all that is allied thereto can manifestly persuade men to great evil, and by writing these verses, even though they should, as the writers of the prefaces think, enkindle the young men of Ireland to hope and activity, Mr Rooney has been persuaded to great evil. And yet he might have written well if he had not suffered from one of those big words which make us so unhappy. There is no piece in the book which has even the first quality of beauty, the quality of integrity, the quality of being separate and whole, but there is one piece in the book which seems to have come out of a conscious personal life. It is a translation of some verses by Dr Douglas Hyde, and is called "A Request," and yet I cannot believe that it owes more than its subject to its original. It begins:—

> In that last dark hour when my bed I lie on,
> My narrow bed of the deal board bare,
> My kin and neighbours around me standing,
> And Death's broad wings on the thickening air.

It proceeds to gather desolation about itself, and does so in lines of living verse, as in the lines that follow. The third line is feeble, perhaps, but the fourth line is so astonishingly good that it cannot be overpraised:—

> When night shall fall and my day is over
> And Death's pale symbol shall chill my face,
> When heart and hand thrill no more responsive,
> Oh Lord and Saviour, regard my case!

And when it has gathered about itself all the imagery of desolation, it remembers the Divine temptation, and puts up its prayer to the Divine mercy. It seems to come out of a personal life which has begun to realise itself but to which death and that realisation have come together. And in this manner, with the gravity of one who remembers all the errors of his members and his sins of speech, it goes into silence.

GEORGE MEREDITH

Review of *George Meredith: An Essay towards Appreciation*,
by Walter Jerrold.

Mr GEORGE MEREDITH has been included in the English men
of letters series, where he may be seen in honourable nearness
to Mr Hall Caine and Mr Pinero. An age which has too keen
a scent for contemporary values will often judge amiss, and,
therefore, one must not complain when a writer who is, even
for those who do not admire him unreservedly, a true man of
letters, comes by his own in such a strange fashion. Mr Jerrold
in the biographical part of his book has to record a more than
usual enormity of public taste, and if his book had recorded
only this, something good would have been done; for it is
certain that the public taste should be reproved, while it is by
no means certain that Mr Meredith is a martyr. Mr Jerrold
confesses his faith in novels and plays alike, and he will have it
that "Modern Love" is on the same plane with the "Vita
Nuova." No one can deny to Mr Meredith an occasional power
of direct compelling speech (in a picture of a famine he wrote
"starving lords were wasp and moth") but he is plainly lacking
in that fluid quality, the lyrical impulse, which, it seems, has
been often taken from the wise and given unto the foolish.
And it is plain to all who believe in the tradition of literature
that this quality cannot be replaced. Mr Meredith's eager brain,
which will not let him be a poet, has, however, helped him to
write novels which are, perhaps, unique in our time. Mr Jerrold
subjects each novel to a superficial analysis, and by doing so he
has, I think, seized a fallacy for his readers. For these novels

have, for the most part, no value as epical art, and Mr Meredith
has not the instinct of the epical artist. But they have a distinct
value as philosophical essays, and they reveal a philosopher at
work with much cheerfulness upon a very stubborn problem.
Any book about the philosopher is worth reading, unless we
have given ourselves over deliberately to the excellent foppery
of the world, and though Mr Jerrold's book is not remarkable,
it is worth reading.

TODAY AND TOMORROW IN IRELAND

Review of *To-day and To-morrow in Ireland*,
by Stephen Gwynn.

IN THIS BOOK, the latest addition to the already formidable
mass of modern Anglo-Irish literature, Mr Gwynn has collected
ten essays from various reviews and journals, essays differing
widely in interest, but for all of which he would claim a unity
of subject. All the essays deal directly or indirectly with Ireland,
and they combine in formulating a distinct accusation of English
civilisation and English modes of thought. For Mr Gwynn,
too, is a convert to the prevailing national movement, and
professes himself a Nationalist, though his nationalism, as he
says, has nothing irreconcilable about it. Give Ireland the status
of Canada and Mr Gwynn becomes an Imperialist at once. It
is hard to say into what political party Mr Gwynn should go,
for he is too consistently Gaelic for the Parliamentarians, and
too mild for the true patriots, who are beginning to speak a
little vaguely about their friends the French. Mr Gwynn,
however, is at least a member of that party which seeks to
establish an Irish literature and Irish industries. The first essays
in his book are literary criticisms, and it may be said at once
that they are the least interesting. Some are mere records of
events and some seem written to give English readers a general
notion of what is meant by the Gaelic revival. Mr Gwynn has
evidently a sympathy with modern Irish writers, but his criticism
of their work is in no way remarkable. In the opening essay
he has somehow the air of discovering Mangan, and
he transcribes with some astonishment a few verses from

"O'Hussey's Ode to the Maguire." Few as the verses are, they
are enough to show the real value of the work of the modern
writers, whom Mr Gwynn regards as the voice of Celticism
proper. Their work varies in merit, never rising (except in Mr
Yeats's case) above a certain fluency and an occasional
distinction, and often falling so low that it has a value only as
documentary evidence. It is work which has an interest of the
day, but collectively it has not a third part of the value of the
work of a man like Mangan, that creature of lightning, who
has been, and is, a stranger among the people he ennobled,
but who may yet come by his own as one of the greatest
romantic poets among those who use the lyrical form.
Mr Gwynn, however, is more successful in those essays which
are illustrative of the industrial work which has been set in
movement at different points of Ireland. His account of the
establishing of the fishing industry in the West of Ireland is
extremely interesting, and so are his accounts of dairies, old-
fashioned and new-fashioned, and of carpet-making. These
essays are written in a practical manner, and though they are
supplemented by many quotations of dates and figures, they
are also full of anecdotes. Mr Gwynn has evidently a sense of
the humorous, and it is pleasing to find this in a revivalist. He
tells how, fishing one day, it was his fortune to meet with
an old peasant whose thoughts ran all upon the traditional
tales of his country and on the histories of great families.
Mr Gwynn's instinct as a fisherman got the better of his
patriotism, and he confesses to a slight disappointment when,
after a good catch on an unfavourable day, he earned no word
of praise from the peasant, who said, following his own
train of thought, "The Clancartys was great men, too. Is there
any of them living?" The volume, admirably bound and printed,
is a credit to the Dublin firm to whose enterprise its publication
is due.

A SUAVE PHILOSOPHY

Review of *The Soul of a People*,
by H. Fielding Hall.

IN THIS BOOK one reads about a people whose life is ordered according to beliefs and sympathies which will seem strange to us. The writer has very properly begun his account of that life by a brief exposition of Buddhism, and he sets forth so much of its history as illustrates its main principles. He omits some incidents which are among the most beautiful of the Buddhist legend—the kindly devas strewing flowers under the horse, and the story of the meeting of Buddha and his wife. But he States at some length the philosophy (if that be the proper name for it) of Buddhism. The Burmese people seem naturally adapted to follow such a wise passive philosophy. Five things are the five supreme evils for them—fire, water, storms, robbers, and rulers. All things that are inimical to human peace are evil. Though Buddhism is essentially a philosophy built against the evils of existence, a philosophy which places its end in the annihilation of the personal life and the personal will, the Burmese people have known how to transform it into a rule of life at once simple and wise. Our civilisation, bequeathed to us by fierce adventurers, eaters of meat and hunters, is so full of hurry and combat, so busy about many things which perhaps are of no importance, that it cannot but see something feeble in a civilisation which smiles as it refuses to make the battlefield the test of excellence. There is a Burmese saying—"The thoughts of his heart, these are the wealth of a man," and Mr Hall, who has lived in Burma for many years, draws a picture of Burmese life which shows that a happiness, founded upon peace of mind in all circumstances, has a high place in the Burmese table of values. And happiness abides among this people: the yellow-robed monks begging alms, the believers coming to tell their beads in the temple, tiny rafts drifting down the river on the night of some festival, each one bearing upon it a tiny lamp, a girl sitting at evening in the shadow of the eaves until the young men come "courting"—all this is part of a suave philosophy which does not know that there is anything to justify tears and lamentations. The courtesies of life are not neglected; anger and rudeness of manners are condemned; the animals themselves are glad to be under masters who treat them as living beings worthy of pity and toleration. Mr Hall is one of the conquerors of this people, and as he does not think it a warrior people he cannot predict for it any great political future. But he knows that peace lies before it, and, perhaps in literature, or in some art, a national temper so serene and order-loving may achieve itself. He gives a version of the story of Ma Pa Da, which he calls "Death the Deliverer," and this story itself is so pitiful that one would wish to know more of the Burmese popular tales. He gives elsewhere a rendering in prose of a Burmese love-song, which has, as may be seen, kept some of its charm, though it has lost, no doubt, much of its music:—

The moon wooed the lotus in the night, the lotus was wooed by the moon, and my sweetheart is their child. The flower opened in the night, and she came forth; the petals moved and she was born.

She is more beautiful than any flower; her face is as delicate as the dusk; her hair is as night falling over the hills; her skin is as bright as the diamond. She is very full of health, no sickness can come near her.

When the wind blows I am afraid, when the breezes move I fear. I fear lest the south wind take her, I tremble lest the breath of evening woo her from me—so light is she, so graceful.

Her dress is of gold, of silk and gold, and her bracelets are of fine gold. She has precious stones in her ears, but her eyes, what jewels can compare unto them?

She is proud, my mistress; she is very proud, and all men are afraid of her. She is so beautiful and so proud that all men fear her.

In the whole world there is none anywhere that can compare unto her.

Mr Hall has written a most pleasing book in an easy and temperate style, a book which is full of interesting manners and stories. One is glad to see that even in these days of novels, religious and sensational, this book has run to four editions.

AN EFFORT AT PRECISION IN THINKING

Review of *"Colloquies of Common People,"*
reported by James Austie [sic].

HE MUST BE a hardy man who contends that the disputants in this book are common people. They are, happily for the peace of human animals, very uncommon people. For common people will not argue for any considerable time as to whether succession of appearances is or is not anything more than the appearance of succession. But these uncommon people, whose colloquies are recorded here at somewhat distressing length by Mr Austie [*sic*], argue about such subtleties with a precision which is more apparent than real. The speakers will seem more precise than they are, for at one time they dispute eagerly over certainty of thought, though certainty is not a habit of the mind at all, but a quality of propositions, and the speakers are really arguing about certitude, and more than once all the speakers are agreed that sense impressions mark the furthest limit of knowledge, and that "reasonable belief" is an oxymoron— conclusions with which the man of the people, who is no philosopher, professes himself in loud accord. However, this book is an effort at precision in thinking, even if it does not always provoke that stimulated attention which one speaker calls a form of activity.

COLONIAL VERSES

Review of *Songs of an English Esau*,
by Clive Phillips-Wolley.

THESE ARE COLONIAL verses. The colonial Esau is asked on page 3 would he change his pottage for Jacob's birthright—a question which evidently expects the answer, No. One piece is named "Is Canada Loyal?" and Mr Wolley proclaims that it is loyal. His verse is for the most part loyal, and where it is not, it describes Canadian scenery. Mr Wolley says that he is a barbarian; he does not want the "murmurous muddle" of the choir; he wants a "clean-cut creed," "plain laws for plain men." There is a piece called "Tableau," about a girl dreaming in a picture gallery. It begins: "I wonder if it's really true that you are only paint."

CATILINA

THE FRENCH TRANSLATORS of this play have included in their preface some extracts from Ibsen's preface to the Dresden edition of 1875 and these extracts tell somewhat humorously the history of Ibsen's early years. The play was written in 1848, when Ibsen was twenty, a poor student working all day in a druggist's shop, and studying during the night as best he could. Sallust and Cicero, it seems, awakened his interest in the character of Catiline, and he set to work to write a tragedy, in part historical and in part political, a reflection of the Norway of his day. The play was politely refused by the directors of the Christiania Theatre and by all the publishers. One of Ibsen's friends, however, published it at his own expense, fully convinced that the play would at once make the writer's name famous in the world. A few copies were sold and, as Ibsen and his friend were in need of money, they were glad to sell the remainder to a pork-butcher. "For some days," Ibsen writes, "we did not lack the necessaries of life." This is a sufficiently instructive history, and it is well to remember it when reading a play which Ibsen publishes simply that his work may be complete. For the writer of *Catilina* is not the Ibsen of the social dramas, but, as the French translators joyfully proclaim, an ardent romantic exulting in disturbance and escaping from all formal laws under cover of an abundant rhetoric. This will not appear so strange when it is remembered that the young Goethe was somewhat given to alchemical researches, and as, to quote Goethe himself, the form in which a man goes into the shadows is the form which he moves among his posterity,

posterity will probably forget Ibsen the romantic as completely as it forgets Goethe and his athanor.

Yet, in some ways, this earlier manner suggests the later manner. In *Catilina* three figures are projected against the background of a restless and moribund society—Catiline, Aurelia, his wife, and Fulvia, a vestal virgin. Ibsen is known to the general public as a man who writes a play about three people—usually one man and two women—and even critics, while they assert their admiration for Ibsen's "unqualified objectivity," find that all his women are the same woman renamed successively Nora, Rebecca, Hilda, Irene—find, that is to say, that Ibsen has no power of objectivity at all. The critics, speaking in the name of the audience, whose idol is common sense, and whose torment is to be confronted with a clear work of art that reflects every obscurity like a mirror, have sometimes had the courage to say that they did not understand the system of three. They will be pleased to learn that some of the characters in *Catilina* are in as sorry a plight as themselves. Here is a passage in which Curius, a young relative of Catiline, professes his inability to understand Catiline's relations with Fulvia and Aurelia:

> CURIUS.   *Les aimerais-tu toutes deux á la fois?*
> *Vraiment je n'y comprends plus rien.*
> CATILINA.   *En effet c'est singulier et je n'y comprends*
> *Rien moi-même.*

But perhaps that he does not understand is part of the tragedy, and the play is certainly the struggle between Aurelia, who is happiness and the policy of non-interference, and Fulvia, who is at first the policy of interference and who, when she has escaped from the tomb to which her sin had brought her, becomes the figure of Catiline's destiny. Very little use is made in this play of alarms and battles, and one can see that the writer is not interested in the usual property of romanticism. Already he is losing the romantic temper when it should be at its fiercest in him, and, as youth commonly brooks no prevention, he is content to hurl himself upon the world and establish himself there defiantly until his true weapons are ready to his hand. One must not take too seriously the solution of the drama in favour of Aurelia, for by the time the last act is reached the characters have begun to mean nothing to themselves and in the acted play would be related to life only by the bodies of the performers. And here is the most striking difference between Ibsen's earlier manner and his later manner, between romantic work and classical work. The romantic temper, imperfect and impatient as it is, cannot express itself adequately unless it employs the monstrous or heroic. In *Catilina* the women are absolute types, and the end of such a play cannot but savour of dogma—a most proper thing in a priest but a most improper in a poet. Moreover, as the breaking up of tradition, which is the work of the modern era, discountenances the absolute and as no writer can escape the spirit of his time, the writer of dramas must remember now more than ever a principle of all patient and perfect art which bids him express his fable in terms of his characters.

As a work of art *Catilina* has little merit, and yet one can see in it what the directors of the Christiania theatre and the publishers failed to see—an original and capable writer struggling with a form that is not his own. This manner continues, with occasional lapses into comedy, as far as *Peer Gynt,* in which, recognising its own limitations and pushing lawlessness to its extreme limit, it achieves a masterpiece. After that it disappears and the second manner begins to take its place, advancing through play after play, uniting construction and speech and action more and more closely in a supple rhythm, until it achieves itself in *Hedda Gabler.* Very few recognise the astonishing courage of such work and it is characteristic of our age of transition to admire the later manner less than the earlier manner. For the imagination has the quality of a fluid, and it must be held firmly, lest it become vague, and delicately, that it may lose none of its magical powers. And Ibsen has united with his strong, ample, imaginative faculty a pre-occupation with the things present to him. Perhaps in time, even the professional critic, accepting the best of the social dramas for what they are—the most excellent examples of skill and intellectual self-possession—will make this union a truism of professional criticism. But meanwhile a young generation which has cast away belief and thrown precision after it, for which Balzac is a great intellect and every sampler who chooses to wander amid his own shapeless hells and heavens a Dante without the unfortunate prejudices of Dante, will be troubled by this pre-occupation, and out of very conscience will denounce a method so calm, so ironical. These cries of hysteria are confused with many others—the voices of war and statecraft and religion—in the fermenting vat. But Boötes, we may be sure, thinks nothing of such cries, eager as ever at that ancient business of leading his hunting-dogs across the zenith "in their leash of sidereal fire."

THE SOUL OF IRELAND

Review of *Poets and Dreamers: Studies and
Translations from the Irish*,
by Lady Gregory.

ARISTOTLE FINDS AT the beginning of all speculation the feeling
of wonder, a feeling proper to childhood, and if speculation
be proper to the middle period of life it is natural that one
should look to the crowning period of life for the fruit of
speculation, wisdom itself. But nowadays people have greatly
confused childhood and middle life and old age; those who
succeed in spite of civilisation in reaching old age seem to have
less and less wisdom, and children who are usually put to some
business as soon as they can walk and talk, seem to have more
and more "common sense;" and, perhaps, in the future little
boys with long beards will stand aside and applaud, while old
men in short trousers play handball against the side of a house.
This may even happen in Ireland, if Lady Gregory has truly set
forth the old age of her country. In her new book she has left
legends and heroic youth far behind, and has explored in a land
almost fabulous in its sorrow and senility. Half of her book is
an account of old men and old women in the West of Ireland.
These old people are full of stories about giants and witches,
and dogs and black-handled knives, and they tell their stories
one after another at great length and with many repetitions (for
they are people of leisure) by the fire or in the yard of a
workhouse. It is difficult to judge well of their charms and
herb-healing, for that is the province of those who are learned
in these matters and can compare the customs of countries,

and, indeed, it is well not to know these magical-sciences, for if the wind changes while you are cutting wild camomile you will lose your mind. But one can judge more easily of their stories. These stories appeal to some feeling which is certainly not that feeling of wonder which is the beginning of all speculation. The story-tellers are old, and their imagination is not the imagination of childhood. The story-teller preserves the strange machinery of fairyland, but his mind is feeble and sleepy. He begins one story and wanders from it into another story, and none of the stories has any satisfying imaginative wholeness, none of them is like Sir John Daw's poem that cried tink in the close. Lady Gregory is conscious of this, for she often tries to lead the speaker back to his story by questions, and when the story has become hopelessly involved, she tries to establish some wholeness by keeping only the less involved part; sometimes she listens "half interested and half impatient." In fine, her book, wherever it treats of the "folk," sets forth in the fullness of its senility a class of mind which Mr Yeats has set forth with such delicate scepticism in his happiest book, "The Celtic Twilight." Something of health and naturalness, however, enters with Raftery, the poet. He had a terrible tongue, it seems, and would make a satirical poem for a very small offence. He could make love-poems, too (though Lady Gregory finds a certain falseness in the western love-poems), and repentant poems. Raftery, though he be the last of the great bardic procession, has much of the bardic tradition about him. He took shelter one day from the rain under a bush: at first the bush kept out the rain, and he made verses praising it, but after a while it let the rain through, and he made verses dispraising it. Lady Gregory translates some of his verses, and she also translates some West Irish ballads and some poems by Dr Douglas Hyde. She completes her book with translations of four one-act plays by Dr Douglas Hyde, three of which have for their central figure that legendary person, who is vagabond and poet, and even saint at times, while the fourth play is called a "nativity" play. The dwarf-drama (if one may use that term) is a form of art which is improper and ineffectual, but it is easy to understand why it finds favour with an age which has pictures that are "nocturnes," and writers like Mallarmé and the composer of "Recapitulation." The dwarf-drama is accordingly to be judged as an entertainment, and Dr Douglas Hyde is certainly entertaining in the "Twisting of the Rope," and Lady Gregory has succeeded better with her verse-translations here than elsewhere, as these four lines may show:—

> I have heard the melodious harp
> On the streets of Cork playing to us:
> More melodious by far I thought your voice,
> More melodious by far your mouth than that.

This book, like so many other books of our time, is in part picturesque and in part an indirect or direct utterance of the central belief of Ireland. Out of the material and spiritual battle which has gone so hardly with her Ireland has emerged with many memories of beliefs, and with one belief—a belief in the incurable ignobility of the forces that have overcome her—and Lady Gregory, whose old men and women seem to be almost their own judges when they tell their wandering stories, might add to the passage from Whitman which forms her dedication, Whitman's ambiguous word for the vanquished—"Battles are lost in the spirit in which they are won."

J. J.

THE MOTOR DERBY

INTERVIEW WITH THE FRENCH CHAMPION
(FROM A CORRESPONDENT)

Paris, Sunday.

IN THE RUE d'Anjou, not far from the Church of the Madeleine, is M Henri Fournier's place of business. "Paris-Automobile"— a company of which M Fournier is the manager—has its headquarters there. Inside the gateway is a big square court, roofed over, and on the floor of the court and on great shelves extending from the floor to the roof are ranged motor-cars of all sizes, shapes, and colours. In the afternoon this court is full of noises—the voices of workmen, the voices of buyers talking in half-a-dozen languages, the ringing of telephone bells, the horns sounded by the "chauffeurs" as the cars come in and go out—and it is almost impossible to see M Fournier unless one is prepared to wait two or three hours for one's turn. But the buyers of "autos" are, in one sense, people of leisure. The morning, however, is more favourable, and yesterday morning, after two failures, I succeeded in seeing M Fournier.

M Fournier is a slim, active-looking young man, with dark reddish hair. Early as the hour was our interview was now and again broken in upon by the importunate telephone.

"You are one of the competitors for the Gordon-Bennett Cup, M Fournier?"

"Yes, I am one of the three selected to represent France."

"And you are also a competitor, are you not, for the Madrid prize?"

"Yes."

"Which of the races comes first—the Irish race or the Madrid race?"

"The Madrid race. It takes place early in May, while the race for the International Cup does not take place till July."

"I suppose that you are preparing actively for your races?"

"Well, I have just returned from a tour to Monte Carlo and Nice."

"On your racing machine?"

"No, on a machine of smaller power."

"Have you determined what machine you will ride in the Irish race?"

"Practically."

"May I ask the name of it—is it a Mercedes?"

"No, a Mors."

"And its horse-power?"

"Eighty"

"And on this machine you can travel at a rate of—?"

"You mean its highest speed?"

"Yes."

"Its highest speed would be a hundred and forty kilometres an hour."

"But you will not go at that rate all the time during the race?"

"Oh, no. Of course its average speed for the race would be lower than that."

"An average speed of how much?"

"Its average speed would be a hundred kilometres an hour, perhaps a little more than that, something between a hundred and a hundred and ten kilometres an hour."

"A kilometre is about a half-mile, is it not?"

"More than that, I should think. There are how many yards in your mile?"

"Seventeen hundred and sixty, if I am right."

"Then your half-mile has eight hundred and eighty yards. Our kilometre is just equal to eleven hundred yards."

"Let me see. Then your top speed is nearly eighty-six miles an hour, and your average speed is sixty-one miles an hour?"

"I suppose so, if we calculate properly."

"It is an appalling pace! It is enough to burn our roads. I suppose you have seen the roads you are to travel?"

"No."

"No? You don't know the course, then?"

"I know it slightly. I know it, that is, from some sketches that were given of it in the Paris newspapers."

"But, surely, you will want a better knowledge than that?"

"Oh, certainly. In fact, before the month is over, I intend to go to Ireland to inspect the course. Perhaps I shall go in three weeks' time."

"Will you remain any time in Ireland?"

"After the race?"

"Yes."

"I am afraid not. I should like to, but I don't think I can."

"I suppose you would not like to be asked your opinion of the result?"

"Hardly."

"Yet, which nation do you fear most?"

"I fear them all—Germans, Americans, and English. They are all to be feared."

"And how about Mr Edge?"

No answer.

"He won the prize the last time, did he not?"

"O, yes."

"Then he should be your most formidable opponent?"

"O, yes . . . But you see, Mr Edge won, of course, but . . . a man who was last of all, and had no chance of winning might win if the other machines broke."

Whatever way one looks at this statement it appears difficult to challenge its truth.

ARISTOTLE ON EDUCATION

Review of *Aristotle on Education*,
Edited by John Burnet.

THIS BOOK IS compiled from the first three books of the Ethics, and the tenth book, with some extracts from the Politics. Unfortunately, the compilation is not a complete treatise on education, nor is it even exhaustive so far as it goes. The Ethics is seized upon by admirers and opponents alike as the weak part of the peripatetic philosophy. The modern notion of Aristotle as a biologist—a notion popular among advocates of "science"—is probably less true than the ancient notion of him as a metaphysician; and it is certainly in the higher applications of his severe method that he achieves himself. His theory of education is, however, not without interest, and is subordinate to his theory of the state. Individualism, it would seem, is not easily recommended to the Greek mind, and in giving his theory of education Aristotle has endeavoured to recruit for a Greek state rather than to give a final and absolute solution to questions of the greatest interest. Consequently this book can hardly be considered a valuable addition to philosophical literature, but it has a contemporary value in view of recent developments in France, and at the present time, when the scientific specialists and the whole cohort of Materialists are cheapening the good name of philosophy, it is very useful to give heed to one who has been wisely named "maestro di color che sauno [*sic*]."

[UNTITLED FRAGMENT]

Review of *"A Ne'er-Do-Weel"* [sic],
by *"Valentine Caryl."*

After all a pseudonym library has its advantages; to acknowledge bad literature by signature is, in a manner, to persevere in evil. "Valentine Caryl's" book is the story of a gypsy genius, whose monologues are eked out by accompaniments on the violin—a story told in undistinguished prose. The series in which this volume appears, the production of the book, and the scantiness of its matter have an air of pretentiousness which is ill justified by perusal.

NEW FICTION

Review of *The Adventures of Prince Aga Mirza*,
by Aquila Kempster.

THIS LITTLE VOLUME is a collection of stories dealing chiefly with Indian life. The reader will find the first five stories—the adventures of Prince Aga Mirza—the most entertaining part of the book, if he is to any extent interested in tales of Indian magic. The appeal, however, of such stories is, frankly, sensational, and we are spared the long explanations which the professional occultists use. The stories that treat of camp life are soundly seasoned with that immature brutality which is always so anxious to be mistaken for virility. But the people who regulate the demand for fiction are being day by day so restricted by the civilisation they have helped to build up that they are not unlike the men of Mandeville's time, for whom enchantments, and monsters, and deeds of prowess were so liberally purveyed.

A book written by the author of "The Increasing Purpose" is sure of a kind hearing from a public which can be thankful to those who serve it well. Mr Allen has not yet written any work of extraordinary merit, but he has written many which are, so far as they go, serious and patient interpretations of his people. Whether it be in the writer or in his theme, one cannot fail to recognise here the quality of self-reliant sanity—the very mettle (to employ the Shakespearian phrase which serves him for the title) of the pasture. The style is nearly always clean and limpid, and is at fault only where it assumes ornateness. The method is psychological, very slightly narrative, and though that epithet has been used to cover a multitude of literary sins, it can be as safely applied to Mr Allen as longo intervallo to Mr Henry James. It is a tragedy of scandal, the story of a love affair, which is abruptly terminated by a man's confession, but which is renewed again years later when it has passed through the trials which the world proposes to such as would renew any association and so offer offence to time and change. This story is surrounded with two or three other love affairs, all more or less conventional. But the characterisation is often very original—as in the case of old Mrs Conyers—and the general current of the book arrests the reader by its suggestion of an eager lively race working out its destiny among other races under the influence of some vague pantheistic spirit which is at times strangely mournful. "For her," he says somewhere in a passage of great charm, "for her it was one of the moments when we are reminded that our lives are not in our keeping, and that whatsoever is to befall us originates in sources beyond our power. Our wills may indeed reach the length of our arms, or as far as our voices can penetrate space; but without us and within us moves one universe that saves us or ruins us only for its own purposes; and we are no more free amid its laws than the leaves of the forest are free to decide their own shapes and seasons of unfolding, to order the showers by which they are to be nourished, and the storms which shall scatter them at last."

A PEEP INTO HISTORY

Review of *The Popish Plot*,
by John Pollock.

ONE MAY HAVE no satirical reference either to the subject of
this book, or to its treatment by Mr Pollock, in saying that this
account of the Popish Plot is far more diverting than many
works of fiction. Mr Pollock, though he seems thoroughly
initiated into the mysteries of the historical method, has set
forth an account of the "Plot" which is clear, detailed, and (so
far as it is critical) liberal-minded. By far the most interesting
part of the book is the story of the murder of Sir Edmund
Godfrey—a murder so artistically secret that it evoked the
admiration of De Quincey, a murder so little documented, yet
so overwhelmed with false testimonies, that Lord Acton declared
it an insoluble mystery. But justice was freely dealt out in those
days of political and religious rancour, and Green and Berry
suffered the last penalty for a crime of which posterity (unanimous
in this one thing at least) has acquitted them. As for those who
swore against the poor wretches, Prauce [*sic*] and Bedloe cannot
be accorded the same condemnation. Prauce [*sic*], after all, was
only lying himself out of a very awkward position, but Bedloe
was a more enterprising ruffian, second only to his monstrous,
moon-faced leader, the horrible Oates. It is bewildering to read
all the charges and counter-charges made in connection with
the Plot, and it is with a sigh of sympathy that we read of
Charles's conduct. "In the middle of the confusion the King
suddenly left for the races at Newmarket, scandalising all by

his indecent levity." Nevertheless he conducted the examination of Oates in a very skilful manner, and he described Oates very succinctly as "a most lying knave." Mr Pollock's treatment of those who have been accused as instigators justifies him in citing a concise phrase from Mabillon on his title page, and the reader will know how patient and scholarly this book is if he compares it with the garbled, ridiculous account set down by L'Estrange.

A FRENCH RELIGIOUS NOVEL

Review of *The House of Sin*,
by Marcelle Tintyre [sic].

THIS NOVEL, REPRINTED from the pages of one of the leading French reviews, and now very successfully translated into English, seems to have attracted more attention in London than in Paris. It deals with the problem of an uncompromising orthodoxy, beset by a peculiarly modern, or (as the Churchmen would say) morbid scepticism, and sorely tried by that alluring, beautiful, mysterious spirit of the earth, whose voice is for ever breaking in upon, and sometimes tempering, the prayers of the saints. Augustine Chanteprie, the descendant of an old Catholic family, many of whose members have been disciples of Pascal, has been brought up in an atmosphere of rigid, practical belief, and is destined, if not for a clerical life, at least for such a life in the world as may be jealously guarded from the snares of the devil, sacrificing as little as may be of innocence and piety. Among his ancestors, however, there was one who forsook the holy counsel given him in youth, and assumed the excellent foppery of the world. He built, in protest against the gloomy house of his family, a pleasant folly, which afterwards came to be known as "The House of Sin." Augustine, unfortunately for himself, inherits the double temperament, and little by little the defences of the spiritual life are weakened, and he is made aware of human love as a subtle, insinuating fire. The intercourse of Augustine and Madame Manole is finely conceived, finely executed, enveloped in a glow of marvellous tenderness. A simple narration has always singular charm when we divine that the lives it offers us are themselves too ample, too complex, to be expressed entirely:—

Augustine and Fanny were now alone. They retraced their steps toward Chene-Pourpre, and suddenly stopping in the middle of the road, they kissed each other . . . There was neither light nor sound. Nothing lived under the vault of heaven but the man and the woman intoxicated by their kiss. From time to time, without disengaging their hands, they drew away and looked at each other.

The last chapters of the book, the chapters in which the tradition of generations overcomes the lover, but so remorselessly that the mortal temple of all those emotions is shattered into fragments, show an admirable adjustment of style and narrative, the prose pausing more and more frequently with every lessening of vitality, and finally expiring (if one may reproduce the impression somewhat fantastically) as it ushers into the unknown, amid a murmur of prayers, the poor trembling soul. The interest in the politico-religious novel is, of course, an interest of the day, and perhaps because Huysmans is daily growing more formless and more obviously comedian in his books that Paris has begun to be wearied by the literary oblate. The writer of "The House of Sin," again, is without the advantage of a perverted career, and is not to be reckoned among the converts. The complication of an innocent male and a woman of the world is, perhaps, not very new, but the subject receives here very striking treatment, and the story gains much by a comparison with Bourget's "Mensonges"—a book that is crude, however detailed and cynical. "Marcelle Tinayre," who seems to have a finer sympathy with Catholicism than most of the neo-Catholics have, is a lover of life and of the fair shows of the world; and though piety and innocence are interwoven with every change of affection and every mood of our manifold nature in these pages, one is conscious that the writer has suspended over her tragedy, as a spectre of sorrow and desolation, the horrible image of the Jansenist Christ.

UNEQUAL VERSE

Review of *Ballads and Legends*,
by Frederick Langbridge.

Mr LANGBRIDGE, IN his preface to this volume of his verses, has confessed to so great a number of literary discipleships that one is well prepared for the variety of styles and subjects of which the book is full. Mr Langbridge's worst manner is very bad indeed; here the worst vices of Browning are united with a disease of sentiment of which the "Master" cannot be justly accused; here "tears splash on ground," blind beggars, mothers' girlies, pathetic clerks, and cripples are huddled together in dire confusion, and the colloquial style, half American half Cockney, is employed to adorn their easily-imagined adventures. Anything more lamentable than the result would be difficult to conceive; and the result is all the more lamentable because the few sonnets which Mr Langbridge has inserted in his volume are evidences of some care and a not inconsiderable technical power. The lines, "To Maurice Maeterlinck," are, therefore, curiously out of place in this farrago of banal epics, so dignified are they in theme, so reserved in treatment, and one can only hope that Mr Langbridge, when he publishes again, will see fit to sacrifice his taste for "comédie larmoyante," and attest in serious verse that love which he professes for the muse.

MR ARNOLD GRAVES'S NEW WORK

Review of *Clytmnæstra [sic]: A Tragedy*,
by Arnold F. Graves.

IN THE INTRODUCTION which Dr Tyrrell has written for Mr
Graves's tragedy, it is pointed out that "Clytemnaestra" [*sic*] is
not a Greek play in English, like "Atalanta in Calydon," but
rather a Greek story treated from the standpoint of a modern
dramatist—in other words it claims to be heard on its own
merits merely, and not at all as a literary curio. To leave aside
for the moment the subordinate question of language it is not
easy to agree with Dr Tyrrell's opinion that the treatment is
worthy of the subject. On the contrary there would appear to
be some serious flaws in the construction. Mr Graves has chosen
to call his play after the faithless wife of Agamemnon, and to
make her nominally the cardinal point of interest. Yet from
the tenor of the speeches, and inasmuch as the play is almost
entirely a drama of the retribution which follows crime, Orestes
being the agent of Divine vengeance, it is plain that the criminal
nature of the queen has not engaged Mr Graves's sympathies.
The play, in fact, is solved according to an ethical idea, and
not according to that indifferent sympathy with certain
pathological states which is so often anathematised by theologians
of the street. Rules of conduct can be found in the books of
moral philosophers, but "experts" alone can find them in
Elizabethan comedy. Moreover, the interest is wrongly directed
when Clytemnaestra, who is about to imperil everything for
the sake of her paramour, is represented as treating him with
hardly disguised contempt, and again where Agamemnon, who

is about to be murdered in his own palace by his own queen on his night of triumph, is made to behave towards his daughter Electra with a stupid harshness which is suggestive of nothing so much as of gout. Indeed, the feeblest of the five acts is the act which deals with the murder. Nor is the effect even sustained, for its second representation during Orestes' hypnotic trance cannot but mar the effect of the real murder in the third act in the mind of an audience which has just caught Clytemnaestra and Egisthus redhanded. These faults can hardly be called venial, for they occur at vital points of the artistic structure, and Mr Graves, who might have sought to cover all with descriptive writing, has been honest enough to employ such a studiously plain language as throws every deformity into instant relief. However, there are fewer offences in the verse than in most of the verse that is written nowadays, and it is perhaps only an indication of the mental confusion incident upon seership when Tiresias, the prophet, is heard exclaiming:

> Beware! beware!
> The stone you started rolling down the hill
> Will crush you if you do not change your course.

A NEGLECTED POET

Review of *George Crabbe*,
by Alfred Ainger.

TENNYSON IS REPORTED to have said that if God made the
country and man made the city, it must have been the devil
that made the country town. The dreary monotonousness, the
squalor, the inevitable moral decay—all, in fine, that has been
called "provincial"—is the constant theme of Crabbe's verse.
Patronised in his own day by Edmund Burke and Charles James
Fox, the friend of Scott, and Rogers, and Bowles, the literary
godfather of FitzGerald, Crabbe has so far fallen in our day
from his high estate that it is only by a favour that he is accorded
mention in some manual of literature. This neglect, though it
can be easily explained, is probably not a final judgment. Of
course, much of Crabbe's work is dull and undistinguished,
and he never had such moments as those which Wordsworth
can always plead in answer to his critics. On the contrary, it is
his chief quality that he employs the metre of Pope so evenly,
and with so little of Pope's brilliancy that he succeeds admirably
as narrator of the obscure tragedies of the provinces. His tales
are, therefore, his claim to a place in the history of English
fiction. At a time when false sentiment and the "genteel" style
were fashionable, and when country life was seized upon for
exploitation as eagerly as by any of the modern Kailyard school,
Crabbe appeared as the champion of realism. Goldsmith had
preceded him in treating rural subjects, treating them with an
Arcadian grace, it is true, but with what remoteness and lack
of true insight and sympathy a comparison of Auburn with

"The Village," "The Borough," and "The Parish Register"
will show. These latter are no more than names in the ears of
the present generation, and it is the purpose of the present
monograph to obtain a hearing, at least, for one of the most
neglected of English writers. The name of its author is one of
the most honourable and painstaking in contemporary criticism,
and amid a multitude of schools and theories perhaps he may
succeed in securing a place for one like Crabbe, who, except
for a few passages wherein the world of opinion is divided, is
an example of sane judgment and sober skill, and who has set
forth the lives of villagers with appreciation and fidelity, and
with an occasional splendour reminiscent of the Dutchmen.

MR MASON'S NOVELS

Review of *The Courtship of Maurice Buckley [sic]*,
The Philanderers, and *Miranda of the Balcony*,
by A. E. W. Mason.

THESE NOVELS, MUCH as they differ in their subjects and styles,
are curiously illustrative of the truth of one of Leonardo's
observations. Leonardo, exploring the dark recesses of
consciousness in the interests of some semi-pantheistic psychology,
has noted the tendency of the mind to impress its own likeness
upon that which it creates. It is because of this tendency, he says,
that many painters have cast as it were a reflection of themselves
over the portraits of others. Mr Mason, perhaps, in like manner,
has allowed these stories to fit themselves into what is doubtless
one of the "moulds of his understanding." Among Mr Mason's
"properties" the reader will not fail to notice the early, effaceable
husband. In "The Courtship of Morrice Buckler" it is Julian
Harwood, in "The Philanderers" it is the outcast Gorley, in
"Miranda of the Balcony" it is Ralph Warriner. In all three books
a previously-implicated girl of wayward habits is associated with
a young man, who is a type of class common enough in novels—
the sturdy, slow-witted Englishman. It is curious to watch this
story reproducing itself without the author's assent, one
imagines, through scenes and times differing so widely. A
minor phenomenon is the appearance of Horace in each story.
In "The Courtship of Morrice Buckler" the plan of the castle
in the Tyrol, which is the centre of gravity of the story, is
made on a page of a little Elzevir copy of Horace. In "The
Philanderers" Horace is laid under tribute more than once for

a simile worthy of the classical beauty of Clarice. And once
again in "Miranda of the Balcony" that interesting figure
"Major" Wilbraham is represented as engaged on a translation
of Horace in the intervals of marauding and blackmailing.
Mr Mason is much more successful when he is writing of a time
or scene somewhat remote from big towns. The Belgravian
atmosphere of "The Philanderers" (a title which Mr Mason has
to share with Mr George Bernard Shaw) is not enlivened by
much wit or incident, but "Miranda of the Balcony" has a pleasing
sequence of Spanish and Moorish scenes. Mr Mason's best book,
however, is certainly "The Courtship of Morrice Buckler." The
story is of the cape and sword order, and it passes in the years
after Sedgemoor. Germany is an excellent place for castles and
intrigues; and in the adventurous air of this romance those who
have read too many novels of modern life may recreate themselves
at will. The writing is often quite pretty, too. Isn't "Miranda of
the Balcony" a pretty name?

THE BRUNO PHILOSOPHY

Review of *Giordano Bruno*,
by J. Lewis McIntyre.

EXCEPT FOR A book in the English or Foreign Philosophical
Library, a book the interest of which was chiefly biographical,
no considerable volume has appeared in England to give an
account of the life and philosophy of the heresiarch martyr of
Nola. Inasmuch as Bruno was born about the middle of the
16th century, an appreciation of him—and that appreciation
the first to appear in England—cannot but seem somewhat
belated now. Less than a third of this book is devoted to
Bruno's life, and the rest of the book to an exposition and
comparative survey of his system. That life reads like a heroic
fable in these days of millionaires. A Dominican monk, a gipsy
professor, a commentator of old philosophies and a deviser of
new ones, a playwright, a polemist, a counsel for his own
defence, and, finally, a martyr burned at the stake in the Campo
dei Fiori—Bruno, through all these modes and accidents (as
he would have called them) of being, remains a consistent
spiritual unity. Casting away tradition with the courage of
early humanism, Bruno has hardly brought to his philosophical
enquiry the philosophical method of a peripatetic. His active
brain continually utters hypotheses; his vehement temper
continually urges him to recriminate; and though the hypothesis
may be validly used by the philosopher in speculation and the
countercheck quarrelsome be allowed him upon occasion,
hypotheses and recriminations fill so many of Bruno's pages
that nothing is easier than to receive from them an inadequate

and unjust notion of a great lover of wisdom. Certain parts of his philosophy—for it is many sided—may be put aside. His treatises on memory, commentaries on the art of Raymond Lally [*sic*], his excursions into that treacherous region from which even ironical Aristotle did not come undiscredited, the science of morality, have an interest only because they are so fantastical and middle aged. As an independent observer, Bruno, however, deserves high honour. More than Bacon or Descartes must he be considered the father of what is called modern philosophy. His system by turns rationalist and mystic, theistic and pantheistic is everywhere impressed with his noble mind and critical intellect, and is full of that ardent sympathy with nature as it is—natura naturata—which is the breath of the Renaissance. In his attempt to reconcile the matter and form of the Scholastics—formidable names, which in his system as spirit and body retain little of their metaphysical character— Bruno has hardly put forward an hypothesis, which is a curious anticipation of Spinoza. Is it not strange, then, that Coleridge should have set him down a dualist, a later Heraclitus, and should have represented him as saying in effect: "Every power in nature or in spirit must evolve an opposite as the sole condition and means of its manifestation; and every opposition is, therefore, a tendency to reunion."? And yet it must be the chief claim of any system like Bruno's that it endeavours to simplify the complex. That idea of an ultimate principle, spiritual, indifferent, universal, related to any soul or to any material thing, as the Materia Prima of Aquinas is related to any material thing, unwarranted as it may seem in the view of critical philosophy, has yet a distinct value for the historian of religious ecstasies. It is not Spinoza, it is Bruno, that is the god-intoxicated man. Inwards from the material universe, which, however, did not seem to him, as to the Neoplatonists, the kingdom of the soul's malady, or as to the Christians a place of probation, but rather his opportunity for spiritual activity, he passes, and from heroic enthusiasm to enthusiasm to unite himself with God. His mysticism is little allied to that of Molinos or to that of St John of the Cross; there is nothing in it of quietism or of the dark cloister: it is strong, suddenly rapturous, and militant. The death of the body is for him the cessation of a mode of being, and in virtue of this belief and of that robust character "prevaricating yet firm," which is an evidence of that belief, he becomes of the number of those who loftily do not fear to die. For us his vindication of the freedom of intuition must seem an enduring monument, and among those who waged so honourable a war, his legend must seem the most honourable, more sanctified, and more ingenuous than that of Averroes or of Scotus Erigena.

HUMANISM

Review of *Humanism: Philosophical Essays*,
by F. S. C. Schiller.

BARBARISM, SAYS PROFESSOR Schiller, may show itself in philosophy in two guises, as barbarism of style and as barbarism of temper, and what is opposed to barbarism is Professor Schiller's philosophical creed: Humanism, or, as he sometimes names it, Pragmatism. One, therefore, who has been prepared to expect courteous humanism both in temper and in style, will read with some surprise statements such as—"The *a priori* philosophies have all been found out;" "Pragmatism . . . has . . . reached the 'Strike, but hear me!' stage," "It [the Dragon of Scholasticism] is a spirit . . . that grovels in muddy technicality, buries itself in the futile burrowings of valueless researches, and conceals itself from human insight [but not from humane insight, Professor Schiller!] by dust-clouds of desiccated rubbish which it raises." But these are details. Pragmatism is really a very considerable thing. It reforms logic, it shows the absurdity of pure thought, it establishes an ethical basis for metaphysic, makes practical usefulness the criterion of truth, and pensions off the Absolute once and for all. In other words, pragmatism is common-sense. The reader, accordingly, will not be surprised to find that in the post-Platonic dialogue, which is called "useless knowledge," a disciple of William James utterly routs and puts to shame the ghostly forms of Plato and Aristotle. Emotional psychology is made the starting-point, and the procedure of the philosopher is to be regulated in accordance. If Professor Schiller had sought to establish rational psychology as a starting-point, his position would have been well-grounded, but rational psychology he has either never heard of or considers unworthy of mention. In his essay on the desire of immortality he establishes one fact—that the majority of human beings are not concerned as to whether or not their life is to end with the dissolution of the body. And yet, after having set up efficiency as the test of truth and the judgment of humanity as the final court of appeal, he concludes by pleading on behalf of the minority, by advocating the claims of the Society for Psychical Research, of which, it seems, he has been for many years a member. Was it so well done, after all, to reform logic so radically? But your pragmatist is nothing if not an optimist, and though he himself denies philosophies by the score, he declares that pessimism is "der Geist der stets verneint." The Mephistopheles of Goethe is the subject of one of the most entertaining essays in the book. "The subtlest of his disguises," says Prof. Schiller in a characteristic sentence, "his most habitual mask, is one which deceives all the other characters in Faust, except the Lord, and has, so far as I know, utterly deceived all Goethe's readers except myself." But surely Professor Schiller can hardly derive much satisfaction from the knowledge that he shares his discovery with the Lord in Goethe's Faust, a being which (to quote the phrase of the English sceptic upon a term of the English sensationalist-theologians) is taken for God because we do not know what the devil it can be, a being, moreover, which is closely allied to such inefficient and pragmatically annihilated entities as the Absolute of Mr Bradley and the Unknowable of Mr Spencer.

SHAKESPEARE EXPLAINED

Review of *Shakespeare Studies in Eight Plays*,
by Hon. A. S. Canning.

IN A SHORT prefatory note the writer of this book states that he has not written it for Shakespearian scholars, who are well provided with volumes of research and criticism, but has sought to render the eight plays more interesting and intelligible to the general reader. It is not easy to discover in the book any matter for praise. The book itself is very long—nearly 500 pages of small type—and expensive. The eight divisions of it are long drawn out accounts of some of the plays of Shakespeare—plays chosen, it would seem, at haphazard. There is nowhere an attempt at criticism, and the interpretations are meagre, obvious, and commonplace. The passages "quoted" fill up perhaps a third of the book, and it must be confessed that the writer's method of treating Shakespeare is (or seems to be) remarkably irreverent. Thus he "quotes" the speech made by Marcellus [*sic*] in the first act of "Julius Caesar," and he has contrived to condense the first 16 lines of the original with great success, omitting six of them without any sign of omission. Perhaps it is a jealous care for the literary digestion of the general public that impels Mr Canning to give them no more than ten-sixteenths of the great bard. Perhaps it is the same care which dictates sentences such as the following:—"His noble comrade fully rivals Achilles in wisdom as in valour. Both are supposed to utter their philosophic speeches during the siege of Troy, which they are conducting with the most energetic ardour. They evidently turn aside from their grand object for a brief space to utter words of profound wisdom . . ." It will be seen that the substance of this book is after the manner of ancient playbills. Here is no psychological complexity, no cross-purpose, no interweaving of motives such as might perplex the base multitude. Such a one is a "noble character," such a one a "villain;" such a passage is "grand," "eloquent," or "poetic." One page in the account of "Richard the Third" is made up of single lines or couplets and such non-committal remarks as "York says then," "Gloucester, apparently surprised, answers," "and York replies," "and Gloucester replies," "and York retorts." There is something very naif about this book, but (alas!) the general public will hardly pay sixteen shillings for such naivete. And the same Philistine public will hardly read five hundred pages of "replies," and "retorts" illustrated with misquotations. And even the pages are wrongly numbered.

[UNTITLED FRAGMENT]

Review of *Borlase and Son*,
by T. Baron Russell.

"BORLASE AND SON" has the merit, first of all, of "actuality." As the preface is dated for May last, one may credit the author with prophetic power, or at least with that special affinity for the actual, the engrossing topic, which is a very necessary quality in the melodramatist. The scene of the story is the suburban district about Peckham Rye, where the Armenians have just fought out a quarrel, and, moreover, the epitasis (as Ben Jonson would call it) of the story dates from a fall of stocks incident upon a revolution among the Latin peoples of America. But the author has an interest beyond that derivable from such allusions. He has been called the Zola of Camberwell, and, inappropriate as the epithet is, it is to Zola we must turn for what is, perhaps, the supreme achievement in that class of fiction of which "Borlase and Son" is a type. In "Au Bonheur des Dames" Zola has set forth the intimate glories and shames of the great warehouse—has, in fact, written an epic for drapers; and in "Borlase and Son," a much smaller canvas, our author has drawn very faithfully the picture of the smaller "emporium," with its sordid avarice, its underpaid labour, its intrigue, its "customs of trade." The suburban mind is not invariably beautiful, and its working is here delineated with unsentimental vigour. Perhaps the unctuousness of old Borlase is somewhat overstated, and the landladies may be reminiscent of Dickens. In spite of its "double-circle" plot, "Borlase and Son" has much original merit, and the story, a little slender starveling of a story, is told very neatly and often very humorously. For the rest, the binding of the book is as ugly as one could reasonably expect.

EMPIRE-BUILDING

EMPIRE-BUILDING DOES NOT appear to be as successful in Northern, as it has been in Southern, Africa. While his cousins are astonishing the Parisian public by excursions in the air M Jacques Lebaudy, the new Emperor of the Sahara, is preparing to venture into the heavier and more hazardous atmosphere of the Palais. He has been summoned to appear today before M André at the suit of two sailors, Jean Marie Bourdiec and Joseph Cambrai, formerly of the *Frosquetta*. They claim 100,000 francs damages on account of the hardships and diseases which they have contracted owing to M Lebaudy's conduct. The new emperor, it would seem, is not over-careful of the bodily welfare of his subjects. He leaves them unprovided-for in a desert, bidding them wait there until he returns. They are made captive by a party of natives and suffer the agonies of hunger and thirst during their captivity. They remain prisoners for nearly two months and are finally rescued by a French man-o'-war under the command of M Jaurès. One of them is subsequently an inmate of a hospital at the Havre and after a month's treatment there is still only convalescent. Their appeals for redress have been all disregarded and now they are having recourse to law. Such is the case of the sailors for the defence of which Maître Aubin and Maître Labori have been retained. The emperor, acting through a certain Benoit, one of his officers, has entered a plea for arbitration. He considers that the case is between the French Republic and the Saharan empire and that in consequence it should be tried before a tribunal of some other nation. He petitions, therefore, that the case should be submitted for judgment to England, Belgium or Holland. However the case goes (and it is plain that the peculiar circumstances attending it render it an extremely difficult one to try) it cannot be that the new empire will gain either materially or in *prestige* by its trial. The dispute, in fact, tends to reduce what was, perhaps, a colonising scheme into a commercial concern but indeed, when one considers how little the colonising spirit appeals to the French people, it is not easy to defend M Lebaudy against the accusation of faddism. The new scheme does not seem to have the State behind it; the new empire does not seem to be entering on its career under any such capable management as reared up the Southern Empire out of the Bechuanaland Commission. But, however this may be, the enterprise is certainly sufficiently novel to excite an international interest in this new candidate for nationhood and the hearing of a case, in which such singular issues are involved, will doubtless divide the attention of the Parisians with such comparatively minor topics as Réjane and *les petits oiseaux*.

(James A. Joyce,
7 S. Peter's Terrace,
Cabra, Dublin)

[UNTITLED FRAGMENT]

. . . . Desire is the feeling which urges us to go to something and loathing is the feeling which urges us to go from something: and that art is improper which aims at exciting these feelings in us whether by comedy or by tragedy. Of comedy later. Tragedy aims at exciting in us feelings of terror and pity. Now terror is the feeling which arrests us before whatever is grave in human fortunes and unites us with its secret cause and pity is the feeling which arrests us before whatever is grave in human fortunes and unites us with the human sufferer. But loathing, which an improper art aims at exciting in the way of tragedy, differs, it is seen, from the feelings which are proper to tragic art, namely, terror and pity. For loathing urges us from rest because it urges us to go from something, but terror and pity hold us in rest, as it were, by fascination. When tragic art makes my body to shrink terror is not my feeling because I am urged from rest; and moreover this art does not show me what is grave, I mean what is constant and irremediable, in human fortunes nor does it unite me with any secret cause for it shows me only what is unusual and remediable in human fortunes and it unites me with a cause only too manifest . . . . Nor is an art properly tragic which would move me to prevent human suffering any more than an art is properly tragic which would move me in anger against some manifest cause of human suffering . . . Terror and pity, finally, are germane to sorrow— the feeling which the privation of some good excites in us . . . .
. . . . And now of comedy. An improper art aims at exciting in the way of comedy the feeling of desire but the

feeling which is proper to comic art is the feeling of joy. Desire, it has been seen, is the feeling which urges us to go to something but joy is the feeling which the possession of some good excites in us. Desire, the feeling which an improper art seeks to excite in the way of comedy, differs, it is seen, from joy. For desire urges us from rest that we may possess something but joy holds us in rest so long as we possess something. Desire, therefore, can be excited in us only by a work of comic art which is not sufficient in itself in as much as it urges us to seek something beyond itself; but a work of comic art which does not urge us to seek anything beyond itself excites in us the feeling of joy. All art which excites in us the feeling of joy is so far comic and according as this feeling of joy is excited by whatever is substantial or accidental, general or fortuitous, in human fortunes the art is to be judged more or less excellent: and even tragic art may be said to participate in the nature of comic art so far as the possession of a work of tragic art excites in us the feeling of joy. From this it may be seen that tragedy is the imperfect manner, and comedy the perfect manner, in art . . . . All art, again, is static for the feelings of terror and pity on the one hand and the feeling of joy on the other hand are feelings which arrest us. Afterwards it will appear how this rest is necessary for the apprehension of the beautiful—the end of all art, tragic or comic,—for this rest is the only condition under which the images, which are to excite in us terror or pity or joy, can be properly presented to us and properly seen by us. For beauty is a quality of something seen but terror and pity and joy are states of mind . . . . . .

J. A. J. 13/2/03. Paris.

. . . . . . There are three conditions of art: the lyrical, the epical and the dramatic. That art is lyrical whereby the artist sets forth the image in immediate relation to himself; that art is epical whereby the artist sets forth the image in mediate [*sic*] relation to himself and to others: that art is dramatic

whereby the artist sets forth the image in immediate relation
to others . . . .

J. A. J. 6 March 1903, Paris.

Rhythm seems to be the first or formal relation of part to part
in any whole or of a whole to its part or parts, or of any part
to the whole of which it is a part . . . Parts constitute a whole
as far as they have a common end.

James A. Joyce, 25 March 1903, Paris

ή τεχνη μιμειται την Φυσιν—This phrase is falsely rendered as
"Art is an imitation of Nature." Aristotle does not here define
art; he says only, "Art imitates Nature" and means that the
artistic process is like the natural process . . . It is false to say
that sculpture, for instance, is an art of repose if by that be
meant that sculpture is unassociated with movement. Sculpture
is associated with movement in as much as it is rhythmic; for
a work of sculptural art must be surveyed according to its
rhythm and this surveying is an imaginary movement in space.
It is not false to say that sculpture is an art of repose in that a
work of sculptural art cannot be presented as itself moving in
space and remain a work of sculptural art.

James A. Joyce, 27 March 1903, Paris

Art is the human disposition of sensible or intelligible matter
for an aesthetic end.

James A. Joyce, 28 March 1903, Paris

Question: *Why are not excrements, children and lice works of art?*
Answer: Excrements, children, and lice are human products—
human dispositions of sensible matter. The process by which

they are produced is natural and non-artistic; their end is not an aesthetic end: therefore they are not works of art.

Question: *Can a photograph be a work of art?*
Answer: A photograph is a disposition of sensible matter and may be so disposed for an aesthetic end but it is not a human disposition of sensible matter. Therefore it is not a work of art.

Question: *If a man hacking in fury at a block of wood make there an image of a cow (say) has he made a work of art?*
Answer: The image of a cow made by a man hacking in fury at a block of wood is a human disposition of sensible matter but it is not a human disposition of sensible matter for an aesthetic end. Therefore it is not a work of art.

Question: *Are houses, clothes, furniture, etc., works of art?*
Answer: Houses, clothes, furniture, etc., are not necessarily works of art. They are human dispositions of sensible matter. When they are so disposed for an aesthetic end they are works of art.

[Pola Notebook]

Bonum est in quod tendit appetitus
S. Thomas Aquinas

The good is that towards the possession of which an appetite tends: the desirable. The true and the beautiful are the most persistent orders of the desirable. Truth is desired by the intellectual appetite which is appeased by the most satisfying relations of the intelligible; beauty is desired by the esthetic appetite which is appeased by the most satisfying relations of the sensible. The true and the beautiful are spiritually possessed, the true by intellection, the beautiful by apprehension; and the appetites which desire to possess them, the intellectual and esthetic appetites, are therefore spiritual appetites.

Pola. J. A. J. 7. XI. 04

Pulcera [*sic*] sunt quae visa placent
S. Thomas Aquinas

Those things are beautiful the apprehension of which pleases. Therefore beauty is that quality of a sensible object in virtue of which its apprehension pleases or satisfies the aesthetic appetite which desires to apprehend the most satisfying relations of the sensible. Now the act of apprehension involves at least two activities, the activity of cognition or simple perception and the activity of recognition. [If] the activity of simple perception is, like every other activity, itself pleasant [,] every sensible object that has been apprehended can be said in the first place to have been and to be in a measure beautiful; and even the most hideous object can be said to have been and to be beautiful in so far as it has been apprehended. In regard then to that part of the act of apprehension which is called the activity of simple perception there is no sensible object which cannot be said to be in a measure beautiful.

With regard to the second part of the act of apprehension which is called the activity of recognition it may further be said that there is no activity of simple perception to which there does not succeed in whatsoever measure the activity of recognition. For by the activity of recognition is meant an activity of decision; and in accordance with this activity in all conceivable cases a sensible object is said to be satisfying or dissatisfying. But the activity of recognition is, like every other activity, itself pleasant and therefore every object that has been apprehended is secondly in whatsoever measure beautiful. Consequently even the most hideous object may be said to be beautiful for this reason as it is *a priori* said to be beautiful in so far as it encounters the activity of simple perception.

Sensible objects, however, are said conventionally to be beautiful or not for neither of the foregoing reasons but rather by reason of the nature, degree and duration of the satisfaction resulting from the apprehension of them and it is in accordance with these latter merely that the words "beautiful" and "ugly" are used in practical aesthetic philosophy. It remains then to be said that these words indicate only a greater or less measure of resultant satisfaction and that any sensible object, to which the word "ugly" is practically applied, an object, that is, the apprehension of which results in a small measure of aesthetic satisfaction, is, in so far as its apprehension results in any measure of satisfaction whatsoever, said to be for the third time beautiful . . .

J. A. J. Pola. 15. XI. 04

The Act of Apprehension

IT HAS BEEN said that the act of apprehension involves at least two activities—the activity of cognition or simple perception and the activity of recognition. The act of apprehension, however, in its most complete form involves three activities— the third being the activity of satisfaction. By reason of the fact that these three activities are all pleasant themselves every sensible object that has been apprehended must be doubly and may be trebly beautiful. In practical aesthetic philosophy the epithets "beautiful" and "ugly" are applied with regard chiefly to the third activity, with regard, that is, to the nature, degree and duration of the satisfaction resultant from the apprehension of any sensible object and therefore any sensible object to which in practical aesthetic philosophy the epithet "beautiful" is applied must be trebly beautiful, must have encountered, that is, the three activities which are involved in the act of apprehension in its most complete form. Practically then the quality of beauty in itself must involve three constituents to encounter each of these three activities . . .

J. A. J. Pola. 16. XI. 04

[UNTITLED FRAGMENT]

To the Editor
17 August 1911   *Via della Barriera Vecchia 32, III,*
                                                    Trieste (Austria)

Sir May I ask you to publish this letter which throws some
light on the present conditions of authorship in England and
Ireland?

Nearly six years ago Mr Grant Richards, publisher, of London
signed a contract with me for the publication of a book of
stories written by me, entitled *Dubliners.* Some ten months later
he wrote asking me to omit one of the stories and passages in
others which, as he said, his printer refused to set up. I declined
to do either and a correspondence began between Mr Grant
Richards and myself which lasted more than three months. I
went to an international jurist in Rome (where I lived then)
and was advised to omit. I declined to do so and the MS was
returned to me, the publisher refusing to publish notwithstanding his pledged printed word, the contract remaining in
my possession.

Six months afterwards a Mr Hone wrote to me from Marseilles
to ask me to submit the MS to Messrs Maunsel, publishers, of
Dublin. I did so: and after about a year, in July 1909, Messrs
Maunsel signed a contract with me for the publication of the
book on or before 1 September 1910. In December 1909 Messrs
Maunsel's manager begged me to alter a passage in one of the
stories, "Ivy Day in the Committee Room," wherein some
reference was made to Edward VII. I agreed to do so, much
against my will, and altered one or two phrases. Messrs Maunsel

continually postponed the date of publication and in the end
wrote, asking me to omit the passage or to change it radically.
I declined to do either, pointing out that Mr Grant Richards
of London had raised no objection to the passage when Edward
VII was alive and that I could not see why an Irish publisher
should raise an objection to it when Edward VII had passed
into history. I suggested arbitration or a deletion of the passage
with a prefatory note of explanation by me but Messrs Maunsel
would agree to neither. As Mr Hone (who had written to me
in the first instance) disclaimed all responsibility in the matter
and any connection with the firm I took the opinion of a
solicitor in Dublin who advised me to omit the passage,
informing me that as I had no domicile in the United Kingdom
I could not sue Messrs Maunsel for breach of contract unless I
paid £100 into court and that, even if I paid £100 into court
and sued them, I should have no chance of getting a verdict
in my favour from a Dublin jury if the passage in dispute could
be taken as offensive in any way to the late king. I wrote then
to the present king, George V, enclosing a printed proof of the
story with the passage therein marked and begging him to
inform me whether in his view the passage (certain allusions
made by a person of the story in the idiom of his social class)
should be withheld from publication as offensive to the memory
of his father. His Majesty's private secretary sent me this reply:

Buckingham Palace

The private secretary is commanded to acknowledge the receipt
of Mr James Joyce's letter of the 1 instant and to inform him
that it is inconsistent with rule for His Majesty to express his
opinion in such cases. The enclosures are returned herewith.

11 August 1911

Here is the passage in dispute:

—But look here, John,—said Mr O'Connor.—Why should
we welcome the king of England? Didn't Parnell himself . . .?—

—Parnell,—said Mr Henchy,—is dead. Now, here's the way I look at it. Here's this chap comes to the throne after his old mother keeping him out of it till the man was grey. He's a jolly fine decent fellow, if you ask me, and no damn nonsense about him. He just says to himself—*The old one never went to see these wild Irish. By Christ, I'll go myself and see what they're like.*—And are we going to insult the man when he comes over here on a friendly visit? Eh? Isn't that right, Crofton?—

Mr Crofton nodded his head.

—But after all now,—said Mr Lyons, argumentatively,—King Edward's life, you know, is not the very . . .—

—Let bygones be bygones.—said Mr Henchy—I admire the man personally. He's just an ordinary knockabout like you and me. He's fond of his glass of grog and he's a bit of a rake, perhaps, and he's a good sportsman. Damn it, can't we Irish play fair?—

I wrote this book seven years ago and, as I cannot see in any quarter a chance that my rights will be protected, I hereby give Messrs Maunsel publicly permission to publish this story with what changes or deletions they may please to make and shall hope that what they may publish may resemble that to the writing of which I gave thought and time. Their attitude as an Irish publishing firm may be judged by Irish public opinion. I, as a writer, protest against the systems (legal, social and ceremonious) which have brought me to this pass. Thanking you for your courtesy, I am, Sir, Your obedient servant

James Joyce

THE CENTENARY OF
CHARLES DICKENS

THE INFLUENCE WHICH Dickens has exercised on the English language (second perhaps to that of Shakespeare alone) depends to a large extent on the popular character of his work. Examined from the standpoint of literary art or even from that of literary craftmanship he hardly deserves a place among the highest. The form he chose to write in, diffuse, overloaded with minute and often irrelevant observation, carefully relieved at regular intervals by the unfailing humorous note, is not the form of the novel which can carry the greatest conviction. Dickens has suffered not a little from too ardent admirers. Before his centenary there was perhaps a tendency to decry him somewhat. Towards the close of the Victorian period the peace of literary England was disturbed by the inroads of Russian and Scandinavian writers inspired by artistic ideals very different from those according to which the literary works (at least of the last century) of the chief writers of fiction had been shaped. A fierce and headstrong earnestness, a resoluteness to put before the reader the naked, nay, the flayed and bleeding reality, coupled with a rather juvenile desire to shock the prim middle-class sentimentalism of those bred to the Victorian way of thinking and writing—all these startling qualities combined to overthrow or, perhaps it would be better to say, to depose the standard of taste. By comparison with the stern realism of Tolstoy, Zola, Dostoiewsky [sic], Bjornson and other novelists of ultra-modern tendency the work of Dickens seemed to have paled, to have lost its freshness. Hence, as I have said, a reaction set in against him and so fickle is popular judgement in literary matters that he was attacked almost as unduly as he had been praised before. It is scarcely necessary to say that his proper place is between these two extremes of criticism; he is neither the great-hearted, great-brained, great-souled writer in whose honour his devotees burn so much incense nor yet the common purveyor of sentimental domestic drama and emotional claptrap as he appears to the jaundiced eye of a critic of the new school.

He has been nicknamed "the great Cockney": no epithet could describe him more neatly nor more fully. Whenever he went far afield to America (as in *American Notes*) or to Italy (as in *Pictures from Italy*) his magic seems to have failed him, his hand seems to have lost her ancient cunning. Anything drearier, and therefore less Dickensian, than the American chapters of *Martin Chuzzlewit* it would be hard to imagine. If Dickens is to move you, you must not allow him to stray out of hearing of the chimes of Bow Bells. There he is on his native heath and there are his kingdom and his power. The life of London is the breath of his nostrils: he felt it as no writer since or before his time felt it. The colours, the familiar noises, the very odours of the great metropolis unite in his work as in a mighty symphony wherein humour and pathos, life and death, hope and despair, are inextricably interwoven. We can hardly appreciate this now because we stand too close to the scenery which he described and are too intimate with his amusing and moving characters. And yet it is certainly by his stories of the London of his own day that he must finally stand or fall. Even *Barnaby Rudge,* though the scene is laid chiefly in London and though it contains certain pages not unworthy of being placed beside the *Journal of the Plague* of Defoe (a writer, I may remark incidentally, of much greater importance than is commonly supposed), does not show us Dickens at his best. His realm is not the London of the time of Lord George Gordon but the London of the time of the Reform Bill. The provinces, indeed the English country of "meadows trim with daisies pied," appear in his work but always as a background or as a preparation. With much greater truth and propriety could Dickens have applied to himself

Lord Palmerston's famous *Civis Romanus sum*. The noble lord, to tell the truth, succeeded on that memorable occasion (as Gladstone, unless my memory misleads me, took care to point out) in saying the opposite of what he had in mind to say. Wishing to say that he was an imperialist he said that he was a Little Englander. Dickens, in fact, is a Londoner in the best and fullest sense of the word. The church bells which rang over his dismal, squalid childhood, over his struggling youth, over his active and triumphant manhood, seem to have called him back whenever, with scrip and wallet in his hand, he intended to leave the city and to have bidden him turn again, like another Whittington, promising him (and the promise was to be amply fulfilled) a threefold greatness. For this reason he has a place for ever in the hearts of his fellow-citizens and also for this reason the legitimate affection of the great city for him has coloured to no slight extent the criticisms passed upon his work. To arrive at a just appreciation of Dickens, to estimate more accurately his place in what we may call the national gallery of English literature it would be well to read not only the eulogies of the London-born but also the opinion of representative writers of Scotland, or the Colonies or Ireland. It would be interesting to hear an appreciation of Dickens written, so to speak, at a proper focus from the original by writers of his own class and of a like (if somewhat lesser) stature, near enough to him in aim and in form and in speech to understand, far enough from him in spirit and in blood to criticize. One is curious to know how the great Cockney would fare at the hands of R.L.S. or of Mr Kipling or of Mr George Moore.

Pending such final judgment we can at least assign him a place among the great literary creators. The number and length of his novels prove incontestably that the writer is possessed by a kind of creative fury. As to the nature of the work so created we shall be safe if we say that Dickens is a great caricaturist and a great sentimentalist (using those terms in their strict sense and without any malice)—great caricaturist in the sense that Hogarth is a great caricaturist, a sentimentalist

in the sense which Goldsmith would have given to that word.
It is enough to point to a row of his personages to see that
he has few (if any) equals in the art of presenting a character,
fundamentally natural and probable with just one strange,
wilful, wayward moral or physical deformity which upsets
the equipoise and bears off the character from the world of
tiresome reality and as far as the borderland of the fantastic.
I should say perhaps the human fantastic, for what figures in
literature are more human and warm-blooded than Micawber,
Pumblechook, Simon Tappertit, Peggoty [*sic*], Sam Weller
(to say nothing of his father), Sara Gamp, Joe Gargery? We
do not think of these, and of a host of others in the well-
crowded Dickensian gallery, as tragic or comic figures or even
as national or local types as we think, for instance, of the
characters of Shakespeare. We do not even see them through
the eyes of their creator with that quaint spirit of nice and
delicate observation with which we see the pilgrims at the
Tabard Inn, noting (smiling and indulgent) the finest and
most elusive points in dress or speech or gait. No, we see
every character of Dickens in the light of one strongly marked
or even exaggerated moral or physical quality—sleepiness,
whimsical self-assertiveness, monstrous obesity, disorderly
recklessness, reptile-like servility, intense round-eyed stupidity,
tearful and absurd melancholy. And yet there are some simple
people who complain that, though they like Dickens very
much and have cried over the fate of Little Nell and over the
death of Poor Joe [*sic*], the crossing-sweeper, and laughed
over the adventurous caprices of Pickwick and his fellow-
musketeers and hated (as all good people should) Uriah Heep
and Fagin the Jew, yet he is after all a *little* exaggerated. To
say this of him is really to give him what I think they call in
that land of strange phrases, America, a billet for immortality.
It is precisely this little exaggeration which rivets his work
firmly to popular taste, which fixes his characters firmly in
popular memory. It is precisely by this little exaggeration that
Dickens has influenced the spoken language of the inhabitants
of the British Empire as no other writer since Shakespeare's
time has influenced it and has won for himself a place deep

down in the hearts of his fellow-countrymen, a honour which has been withheld from his great rival Thackeray. And yet is not Thackeray at his finest greater than Dickens? The question is an idle one. English taste has decreed to Dickens a sovereign position and Turk-like will have no brother near his throne.

James Joyce B. A.

POLITICS AND CATTLE DISEASE

THOUGH THE COUNTRY has not been deceived by the pitiable endeavours of Unionists and factionists to make political capital out of the national calamity involved in the outbreak of the foot and mouth disease in a few Irish districts, Mr Dillon renders a valuable service by pointing out the injury done by the dishonest clamour in which the mischief-makers have indulged. They have, he points out, played into the hands of English Protectionists like Mr Henry Chaplin and Mr Bathurst, whose object is not the security of English herds, but the prolonged exclusion of Irish cattle from the English markets. By enabling such enemies of the Irish farmer to raise the cry that any relaxation of the restrictions that may be proposed is due, not to Mr Runciman's unbiased opinion that the conditions justify the relaxation, but to "Irish dictation," they have simply raised fresh obstructions to the fair treatment of the Irish stock-owners and traders' claims. All these stupid threats and calls upon the Irish Party to "turn out the government" have been ammunition to the English exclusionists. We have seen how the *Globe* has turned them to account. It will have been noticed, too, that none of these Unionist fire-eaters have appealed to their own party for assistance in the matter. According to the London correspondent of the *Irish Times,* "Irish members of all shades of opinion are asking for the removal of restrictions, but without success." This will be news to most people. Hitherto Irish members of the Unionist shade of opinion have been only remarkable for their silence on the matter. Not one of the Irish Unionist Party attended the deputation to Mr Runciman. Mr Chaplin and Mr Bathurst have been allowed to rampage without a word of protest from an Irish Unionist member. Yet the Unionist landlords, land agents, and eleven-months' men, and the defeated factionist candidates who have been joining in their cry, have not addressed a word of protest or appeal to the Irish Unionist leaders to put a snaffle on Mr Chaplin. The simple fact is sufficient to explain the motives and purpose of all the Unionist talk upon the matter.

Mr Dillon points out what would be the certain consequence of action of the kind recommended to the Irish Party. Not only would it involve the sacrifice of the Home Rule Bill and the Home Rule movement, but it would defeat the very object alleged by these advisers. After such an incident no British Minister dare open the English ports for months, because his motives would be instantly challenged. Equally bad and dangerous has been the talk about the unimportance of the disease, and the advice given by some foolish people to the farmers to conceal it. Fortunately the Irish farmers have not listened to the advice. They have proved their commonsense by reporting every suspicious case. Their anxiety to assist the public authorities has been proved by the fact that a majority of the cases so reported have proved to be cases of some other ailment. It is obvious that only by such action can the confidence of the trading public be so restored that the English minister will be free to act upon the facts disclosed. The talk that the disease is only "like measles in children and that all the cattle should be allowed to get it," like the foolish advice to farmers to conceal cases of the disease, is probably the explanation of the extraordinary official suggestion that the healthy areas should be denied their rights "until the situation disclose itself further." The situation is fully disclosed, because the Irish stock-owners have been perfectly above-board in the matter. They ought not to be held responsible for the stupidities of irresponsible speakers like those whom we have quoted. But a moment's reflection will convince the stock-owners that stupid people of the kind are worth as much as ten outbreaks of the disease to persons like the Right Hon. Henry Chaplin and Mr Charles Bathurst.

We do not mean to urge that the Irish farmers and traders should relax their efforts or cease their agitation. Quite the contrary. The situation is critical, and they have sound and solid reasons for demanding the reopening of the ports to healthy Irish stock. These sound and solid reasons are only weakened by menaces that defeat themselves, and by declarations that allow slanderers to say that the disease is being concealed in Ireland. The stock-owners can point to the fact that since the original outbreak, when the existence of the disease could scarcely have been suspected, not a single prosecution for concealment has taken place, though the Constabulary and the officials of the Department are actively watching for symptoms of the disease all over the country. A fact of that kind is the most complete justification of the demand for equality of treatment with the English healthy areas, which the Irish stock-owners and traders are pressing. In putting forward that demand they have the full and hearty co-operation of the Irish Party and its leader. The influence of the party will be exercised no less strongly, because it is being used in a legitimate and reasonable way, and in a manner that will leave the exclusionists with no ground for slander. The Irish Department is, we have the strongest grounds for believing, no less active. Mr Russell has not concealed his endorsement of the claim of the Irish stock-owners. On the contrary, he has taken the strong step of publicly proclaiming his agreement. His statement is the best justification for a vigorous agitation against the unreasonable prolongation of the embargo. It is essential to maintain that agitation, but it is no less essential to discountenance the use of silly and mischievous language, which is the only justification the intimidators of Mr Runciman can plead for their attitude.

PROGRAMME NOTES FOR THE ENGLISH PLAYERS

THE TWELVE POUND LOOK
BY J. M. BARRIE

ONE SIMS IS about to be knighted: possibly, as the name would suggest, for having patented a hairgrower. He is discovered rehearsing his part with his wife whose portrait we see on the wall, painted by a Royal Academician, also knighted, presumably for having painted the label for the hairgrower. A typist is announced. This typist is his runaway wife of some fourteen years before. From their conversation we learn that she left him not for another man but to work out her salvation by typewriting. She had saved twelve pounds and bought a typewriter. The twelve pound look, she says, is that look of independence in a wife's eye which every husband should beware of. The new knight's new wife, "noted for her wit"—chary of it, too—seems likely to acquire the look if given time. Typewriters, however, are rather scarce at present.

RIDERS TO THE SEA
BY JOHN M. SYNGE

SYNGE'S FIRST PLAY, written in Paris in 1902 out of his memories of Aran. The play shows a mother and her dead son, her last, the αναγκη being the inexorable sea which claims all her sons. Seamus and Patch and Stephen and Shaun. Whether a brief tragedy be possible or not (a point on which Aristotle had some doubts) the ear and the heart mislead one gravely if this brief scene from "poor Aran" be not the work of a tragic poet.

THE DARK LADY OF THE SONNETS
BY G. B. SHAW

Mr SHAW HERE presents three orthodox figures—a virgin queen, a Shakespeare sober at midnight and a free giver of gold, and the dark-haired maid of honour, Mary Fitton, discovered in the eighties by Thomas Tyler and Mr Harris. Shakespeare comes to Whitehall to meet her and learns from a well-languaged beefeater that Mr W. H. has forestalled him. The poet vents his spleen on the first woman who passes. It is the queen and she seems not loth to be accosted. She orders the maid of honour out of the way. When Shakespeare, however, begs her to endow his theatre she refers him with fine cruelty to her lord treasurer and leaves him. The most regicide of playwrights prays God to save her and goes home weighing against a lightened purse, love's treason, an old queen's leer and the evil eye of a government official, a horror still to come.

THE HEATHER FIELD
BY EDWARD MARTYN

EDWARD MARTYN, THE author of the "Heather Field," has in company with W. B. Yeats inaugurated the Irish National Theatre. He is an accomplished musician and man of letters. As a dramatist he follows the school of Ibsen and therefore occupies a unique position in Ireland, as the dramatists writing for the National Theatre have chiefly devoted their energies to peasant drama. The plot of the "Heather Field," the best known of Martyn's plays, is as follows:

Carden Tyrrell has made an unhappy marriage early in his youth and is now living on bad terms with his wife, Grace. He is an idealist who has never cared for the ordinary routine of life. Forced to settle down on his estate and finding most of his neighbours uncongenial, he has idealised farming and is engaged at the opening of the play in trying to bring into cultivation a vast tract of heather land. To carry on this work he has had to borrow large sums of money. His friend Barry Ussher and his brother Miles warn him of the danger he is running, but in vain. They urge that he is likely to get little profit from his work, for Ussher knows that it is very hard to reclaim lands on which heather grows, for the wild heather may break out upon them soon again. Grace learns that Carden intends borrowing further large sums of money and fears that he will ruin himself. Carden has admitted to his brother Miles that he hears mysterious voices in the air and that every day life is becoming more and more unreal to him. Convinced that he has lost his reason, Grace confides to her friend, Lady Shrule, that she has arranged for two doctors to come and see Carden; she hopes to have him certified as a lunatic and put under restraint. Lady Shrule sympathises, but neither she nor her husband will do anything to help. The doctors come on an excuse of examining Kit, Carden's son, but the plan is defeated by Barry Ussher who warns them of the danger they are running by falling in with Grace's scheme. However matters go from bad to worse; Carden quarrels with his tenants, thus losing further money and having to have police protection. He is unable to pay the interest on the sums he has borrowed and is threatened with financial ruin. At this crisis Kit comes back from a ride and shows his father some wild heather buds which he has found in the heather field. Carden loses his reason and memory; his mind goes back to happy days before his marriage. As Grace tried to domesticate him, so he has tried to domesticate the heather field, and in each case the old wild nature avenges itself.

FROM A BANNED WRITER TO A
BANNED SINGER

HE STRIDES, BOOTED with anger, along the spurs of Monte Rossini, accompanied solely by Fidelion, his mastiff's voice. They quarrel consonantly about the vocality of the wind, calling each and its other clamant names.

*

Just out of kerryosity howlike is a Sullivan? It has the fortefaccia of a Markus Brutas, the wingthud of a spreadeagle, the body uniformed of a metropoliceman with the brass feet of a collared grand. It cresces up in Aquilone but diminuends austrowards. It was last seen and heard of by some macgilliccuddies above a lonely valley of their reeks, duskening the greylight as it flew, its cry echechohoing among the anfractuosities: *pour la dernière fois!* The blackbulled ones, stampeding, drew in their horns, all appailed and much upset, which explaints the guttermilk on their overcoats.

*

A pugilant gang theirs, per Bantry! Don Philip, Jay Hell, Big O'Barry of the Bornstorms, Arthur, siruraganist who loosed that chor. Damnen. And tramp, tramp, tramp. And T. Deum sullivamus.

Faust of all, of curse, damnation. But given Parigot's Trocadéro for his drawingroom with Ballaclavier in charge at the pianone the voice becomes suburban, sweethearted and subdued. The heat today was really too much of a hot thing

145

and even Impressario is glad to walk his garden in the cool of the evening, fanning his furnaceface with his sweltertails. *Merci, doux crépuscule!*

*

Who is this that advances in maresblood caftan, like Hiesous in Finisterre, his eyeholes phyllistained, his jewbones of a crossbacked? A little child shall lead him. Why, it's Strongman Simpson, Timothy Nathan, now of Simpson's on the Grill! Say, Tim Nat, bald wine-presser, hast not one air left? But yeth he hath. Regard! Auscult! He upbraces for supremacy to the potence of Mosthigh and calls upon his baiters and their templum: You daggones, be flat!

*

What was in that long long note he just delivered? For the laib of me I cannot tell. More twopenny tosh and luxus languor about I singabob you? No such thing, O son of an envelope. Dr to J. S. Just a pennyplain loafletter from Braun and Brotmann and it will take no rebutter. You may bark Mrs Liebfraumich as long as you love but you must not burk the baker. Pay us disday our daily bread. And oblige.

*

On his native heath. Speech! Speech! cry the godlets. We are in land of Dan. But their words of Muskerry are harsh after that song of Othello. *Orateur ne peut, charlatan ne daigne, Sullivan est.*

*

11.59 p.m. *Durch diese hohle Gasse muss er kommen.* Guillaume's shot telled, sure enough. But will that labour member for Melckthal be able to bring off his coo for the odd and twentieth supererogatory time? *Wartemal!* That stagesquall has passed over like water off a Helvetian's back. And there they are, yodelling yokels, none the worse for their ducking and *gewittermassen* as free as you fancy to quit their homeseek *heimat* and leave the ritzprinz of their chyberschwitzerhoofs all over both worlds, cisalpic and transatlantine. And how confederate of gay old Gioacchino to have composed this finale so that Kamerad Wagner might be saved the annoyance of finding flauts for his *Feuerzauber! Pass auf!* Only four bars more! He draws the breathbow: that arrownote's coming. Aim well, Arnold, and mind puur blind Jemmy in the stalls! But, great Scott, whas is thas for a larm! Haif a ton of brass in the band, ten thousand throats from Thalwyl: Libertay. libertay lauded over the land. (Tay!) And pap goes the Calville!

*

Saving is believing but can thus be? Is this our model vicar of Saint Wartburgh's, the reverend Mr Townhouser, Mus. Bac., discovered flagrant in a *montagne de passe?* She is obvious and is on her three-legged sofa in a half yard of casheselks, Madame de la Pierreuse. How duetonically she hands him his harp that once, bitting him, whom caught is willing: do blease to, fickar! She's as only roman as any *puttana madonna* but the trouble is that the reverend T is reformed. She, *simplicissima,* wants her little present from the reverend since she was wirk worklike never so nice with him. But he harps along about Salve Regina Terrace and Liza, mine Liza, and sweet Marie. Till she cries: bilk! And he calls: blak! O.u.t. spells out!

*

Since we are bound for a change of supper, was that really in faith the reverend Townhouser for he seemed so verdamnably like? *Ecco trovato!* Father Lucullus Ballytheacker, the parish priest of Tarbert. He was a songful soul at the keyboard and could achieve his Château Kirwan with cigar thuriferant, without ministrance from platform or pulpit, chase or church. Nor used he to deny his Mary neither. *Nullo modo.* Up to maughty London came a muftimummed P.P. Censored.

★

Have you got your knife handy? asks the bellman Saint Andy. Here he is and brandnew, answers Bartholomew. Get ready, get ready, scream the bells of Our Lady. And make sure they're quite killed, adds the gentle Clotilde. Your attention, sirs, please, bawls big Brother Supplice. *Pour la foi! Pour la foi!* booms the great Auxerrois.

Grand spectacular exposition of gorge cutting, mortarfiring and general martyrification, bigleighted up with erst classed instrumental music. *Pardie!* There's more sang in that Sceine than mayer's beer at the Guildhall. Is he a beleaper in Irisk luck? Can he swhipstake his valentine off to Dublin and weave her a frock of true blue poplin to be neat for the time Hugenut Cromwell comes over, gentlest lovejesus as ever slit weasand? Their cause is well sainted and they are centain to won. Still I'll pointe half my crown on Raoul de Nangis, doublet mauve and cuffs of buff. Attagirl! *Ah ah ah ah ah ah viens!* Piffpaff, but he's done it, the bully mastiff again. And woops with him through the window tallyhoed by those friers pecheurs who are selfbarked. Dominie's canes. Can you beat that, you papish yelpers? To howl with the pups!

★

Enrico, Giacomo and Giovanni, three dulcetest of our songsters, in liontamers overcoats, holy communion ties and cliqueclaquehats, are met them at a gaslamp. It is kaputt and throws no light at all on the trio's tussletusculums. Rico is for carousel and Giaco for luring volupy but Nino, the sweetly dulcetest, tuningfork among tenors, for the best of all; after hunger and sex comes dear old *somnium,* brought on by prayer.

Their lays, blent of feastings, June roses and ether, link languidly in the unlit air. Arrives a type in readymade, dicky and bowler hat, manufactured by Common Sense and Co. Ltd., carrying a bag of tools. Preludingly he conspews a portugaese into the gutter, recitativing: now then, gents, by your leave! And, to his job. Who is this hardworking guy? No one but Geoge, Geoge who shifts the garbage can, Geoge who stokes in the engine room, Geoge who has something to say to the gas (*tes gueules!*) and mills the wheel go right go round and makes the world grow lighter. *Lux!* The aforesung Henry. James and John stand mouthshut. Wot did I say? Hats off *primi assoluti!* Send him canorious, long to lung over us, high topseasoarious! Guard safe our Geoge!